The Basic Plan *for the* Ongoing Formation *of* Priests

UNITED STATES CATHOLIC CONFERENCE
Washington, D.C.

The Basic Plan for the Ongoing Formation of Priests, which was prepared by the Bishops' Committee for Priestly Life and Ministry, was first reviewed by the body of bishops during and subsequest to their General Meeting in November 1999. The plan was also reviewed by the diocesan directors for the continuing education of priests in each of the thirteen episcopal regions of the United States, with the assistance of the National Organization for the Continuing Education of Roman Catholic Clergy. In June 2000, the National Conference of Catholic Bishops approved the plan as a set of guidelines for the development of local programs for the ongoing formation of priests. The plan was then reviewed by the Congregation for the Clergy and is authorized for publication by the undersigned.

Monsignor William P. Fay
General Secretary
NCCB/USCC

Also available in Spanish: pub. no. 5-845

ISBN 1-57455-383-6

First Printing, June 2001

Contents

CONGREGATIO
PRO CLERICIS

Vatican City, 7 February 2001

National Conference of Catholic Bishops
3211 Fourth Street NE
Washington, DC 20017-1194
U.S.A.

My Dear Brothers,

It is with joy that I write to you regarding the publication of the *National Plan for the Ongoing Formation of Priests*. As Prefect of the Congregation for the Clergy, the Dicastery with this particular responsibility, I am most grateful for the efforts that you have made in this area.

Ongoing formation is a vital and necessary aspect of the life of a priest. It should be considered as a basic part of priestly activity and as such should be given the attention and resources needed to ensure that all priests may have access to it. It is through this ongoing formation that we as priests can be totally attuned to the teaching and thought of the Church and thus appropriately respond to the needs of our people.

I hope that in conjunction with the existing documents issued by this Congregation namely, *The Directory on the Ministry and Life of Priests*, the inter-Dicasterial document *On Certain Questions Regarding the Collaboration of the Non-Ordained Faithful in the Sacred Ministry of Priests* and *The Priest and the Third Christian Millennium*, this contribution will help further the formation of priests.

I am encouraged by your activity in this area and wish your plan every success in its reception and implementation.

Please be assured of my prayerful support, I remain,

Yours sincerely in Christ,

Darío Cardinal Castrillón Hoyos
PREFECT

Abbreviations Used in This Plan

CL *The Vocation and the Mission of the Lay Faithful in the Church and in the World (Christifideles Laici)*

DMLP *The Directory on the Ministry and Life of Priests*

EA *The Church in America (Ecclesia in America)*

GS *Pastoral Constitution on the Church in the Modern World (Gaudium et Spes)*

LG *Dogmatic Constitution on the Church (Lumen Gentium)*

NCCB National Conference of Catholic Bishops

NOCERCC National Organization for the Continuing Education of Roman Catholic Clergy

PDV *I Will Give You Shepherds (Pastores Dabo Vobis)*

PO *Decree on the Ministry and Life of Priests (Presbyterorum Ordinis)*

PPF *Program of Priestly Formation*

USCC United States Catholic Conference

Foreword

We recognize the jubilee time of the new millennium as a special opportunity for conversion and spiritual renewal for the Church in general and for our priests in particular. With that in mind, we offer this *Basic Plan for the Ongoing Formation of Priests*. We hope that this *ratio fundamentalis* or basic plan will provide an impetus for ongoing formation and a catalyst for program development.

This document seeks to complement the directions set out in the apostolic exhortation *I Will Give You Shepherds* (*Pastores Dabo Vobis*) (PDV) of His Holiness, Pope John Paul II, and in *The Directory on the Ministry and Life of Priests* (DMLP) developed by the Congregation for the Clergy. This *Basic Plan for the Ongoing Formation of Priests* can complement and follow up the *Program of Priestly Formation* currently in use in the United States.

We propose this document for the ongoing formation for priests as a guide for the next ten years. We are mindful that the majority of those who will make up our presbyterates in the next ten years are already priests, and thus, will benefit from the directions in this document.

We recognize the special and unique formational needs of members of religious congregations. This document is aimed more specifically to members of diocesan presbyterates. We invite those responsible for the ongoing formation of members of religious congregations to study this document and to make useful applications where possible. We hope that the episcopal conference will periodically renew this plan.

We are grateful to many people for their work in developing this document. I would like to express our thanks to the members of the Priestly Life and Ministry Committee who have spent many hours in reviewing this work. They are as follows: Bishop Francis J. Christian, Bishop John R. Gaydos, Bishop George H. Niederauer, Bishop William S. Skylstad, Bishop Arthur Tafoya, and Bishop Paul A. Zipfel. Consultants to the committee are the following: Very Rev. Frederick P. Annie, Rev. Msgr. Timothy Dyer, Very Rev. Robert F. Guay, Rev. William D. Hammer, Rev. Charles Latus, Rev. Frank Reale, SJ, Rev. Kevin J. Spiess, Rev. Francis Tebbe, OFM, and Rev. Donald Wolf. I would like to thank the other readers and members of the National Organization for the Continuing Education of Roman Catholic Clergy (NOCERCC) for their participation in our consultations. I wish also to extend special thanks to Bishop George H. Niederauer and the members of the writing committee for the document. These members are Rev. Louis Cameli, Very Rev. Frederick P. Annie, Very Rev. John Canary, Rev. Noah Casey, OSB, Rev. Clete Kiley, Ms. Mary Ann Pobicki, Rev. Stephen Rossetti, Rev. Francis Tebbe, OFM, Rev. Edward Upton, Rev. Raymond Webb, and Rev. Donald Wolf. I want to acknowledge the particular work of Rev. Louis Cameli who has served as the principal writer and as the general editor of the document. I want to thank Rev. Clete Kiley, the executive director of the Secretariat for Priestly Life and Ministry, for developing this project and keeping it on track. Finally, I want to express our gratitude to the Raskob Foundation for a generous grant that has made this project possible.

It is our hope that this document will be studied by bishops, priests, and seminarians throughout the United States. We call upon individual presbyterates, through their priests' councils, to give special attention to the implementation of the principles contained here. We also call upon national organizations, such as NOCERCC, and the various centers for ongoing formation throughout the country to develop programs, conferences, retreats, symposia, and convocations that carry the principles outlined here forward to implementation. For our part, we as bishops commit ourselves anew to this important work of ongoing formation.

Most Rev. Richard Hanifen
Bishop of Colorado Springs
Chairman, Bishops' Committee for Priestly Life and Ministry

The Commitment of the Bishops of the United States to the Ongoing Formation of Priests

We, the bishops of the United States, have heard the words of our Holy Father Pope John Paul II: "*The entire particular Church* has the responsibility, under the guidance of the Bishop, to develop and look after the different aspects of her priests' permanent formation" (PDV, no. 78).

We understand, again in light of the Holy Father's words to us, that our responsibility for the ongoing formation of priests is rooted in our sacramental relationship with our respective presbyterates: "The Bishop's responsibility is based on the fact that priests receive their priesthood from him and share his pastoral solicitude for the People of God. He is responsible for ongoing formation, the purpose of which is to ensure that all his priests are generously faithful to the gift and ministry received, that they are priests such as the People of God wishes to have and has a 'right' to" (PDV, no. 79).

In obedient response to the Holy Father's express wishes, we commit ourselves to supplying the necessary personnel, time, and finances to make the ongoing formation of priests an effective reality in the life of our dioceses. We will do our best in our respective dioceses. We will also join forces regionally and nationally, when that kind of collective and collaborative effort and investment will better serve the purpose of ongoing formation for priests.

We commit ourselves to reminding our priests of the importance of ongoing formation. We will encourage them in their efforts, and we will call them to accountability in the name of the Church. Furthermore, we will support our priests by informing the entire people of God that the prayer and study of their priests is not something added on to their work but rather is integral to their ministry.

Finally, we commit ourselves to participating in the process of ongoing formation. The Holy Father has said, "The Bishop will live up to his responsibility, not only by seeing to it that his presbyterate has places and times for its ongoing formation, but also by being present in person and taking part in an interested and friendly way" (PDV, no. 79).

Through the intercession of Mary, mother of priests and the great "sign of certain hope and comfort to the pilgrim people of God" (*Dogmatic Constitution on the Church [Lumen Gentium] [LG],* no. 68), we ask God's blessings on all our priests. May they grow in wisdom and grace and, through a new evangelization, draw all people to the Lord Jesus Christ in whose name and person they act and exist.

Part One

THE BASIC PLAN

A. Introduction: A Document About Transformation and Formation

Now the Lord is the Spirit, and where the Spirit of the Lord is, there is freedom. All of us, gazing with unveiled face on the glory of the Lord, are being transformed into the same image from glory to glory, as from the Lord who is the Spirit.

(2 COR 3:17-18)

The apostle Paul marvels at the work of the Holy Spirit who transforms believers into the very image of Jesus Christ, who himself is the image of God. This grace of the new covenant embraces all who have joined themselves to Jesus Christ in faith and baptism. Indeed, it is sheer grace, all God's doing. Moved by that grace, however, we make ourselves available to God's work of transformation. And that making ready a place for the Lord to dwell in us and transform us we call formation.

This document is the basic plan of ongoing formation for priests who count themselves among other believers but who also stand and serve in a unique way in the Church of Christ, conformed to Christ as his sacramental representatives in the presbyteral order. God invites them to transformation across their lifetime, and their formation is marked by constant elements at every stage of life. At the same time, there are specific formational challenges that emerge in particular seasons of their priestly ministry. Both the constant and the changing elements of formation are included in the basic plan.

There is a temptation to use a basic plan to establish an ideal type of priest, an unrealistic, unattainable, and therefore unhelpful goal. A more realistic aim is to identify the true formative points of human, intellectual, spiritual, and pastoral encounter that priests must face in their ministry and lives and that are the privileged places where God's transforming grace touches them.

A basic plan of formation ought to be comprehensive, systematic, practical, and rooted in the Gospel. A comprehensive plan describes the wide range of priestly ministry and life, noting the possibilities of grace and the shadow dimensions of temptation and sin as well as the challenges and resources that are available. A systematic plan organizes the particular elements in ways that connect them together. It draws out practical implications, especially for program development. From the Gospel comes the light and fire of God's love.

At the beginning, it is important to identify the intended audience for a basic plan of priestly formation. Who belongs to this audience? In the first place, the audience includes bishops and presbyterates who want some guidance in the formation of a holy and effective presbyterate, and holy and effective priests. The audience will also include directors of ongoing formation and continuing education who can use this document to organize and review their efforts. Individual priests can also use a basic plan to name their experience and needs and, then, develop a personalized process of ongoing formation. Seminary formation directors and seminarians can use the plan in preparation for priestly ministry. Finally, a basic plan of priestly formation can be a help to the people of God as they seek to support and encourage their priests in their priestly service and spiritual journeys.

In the end, a basic plan of priestly formation ought to inspire and challenge priests to respond to the promptings of God's grace. This means to respond to priests' formational needs in a way that is timely, practical, and specific. In other words, it locates the priestly formation in the United States at the beginning of a new century.

B. Introduction: The Organization of a Basic Plan of Priestly Formation

This plan of ongoing formation for priests in the United States includes two parts. The first treats ongoing formation in a "synchronic" way, noting that there are elements or dynamics of ongoing formation that are the same at every moment of priests' lives. In *Pastores Dabo Vobis*, Pope John Paul II notes, "Permanent or ongoing formation, precisely because it is 'permanent,' should *always* be a part of the priest's life. In every phase and condition of his life, at every level of responsibility he has in the Church, he is undergoing formation" (PDV, no. 76).

The second part of the plan proceeds "diachronically" or longitudinally, identifying the different formational tasks appropriate in the different ages and special moments of priestly ministry and life. Specific attention will be given to the newly ordained, priests in transition, priests entering their first pastorate, priests in midlife, and priests in the third age. A final section considers the formation of an entire presbyterate.

Both the synchronic and diachronic parts of the plan are inspired by and seek to be faithful to the documents of the Second Vatican Council, other significant church documents—especially *Pastores Dabo Vobis: On the Formation of Priests in the Circumstances of the Present Day* (1992), the *Directory on the Ministry and Life of Priests* (Congregation for the Clergy, 1994), *The Church in America (Ecclesia in America): On the Encounter with the Living Jesus Christ: The Way to Conversion, Communion, and Solidarity in America* (EA) (1999), and *The Priest and the Third Christian Millennium: Teacher of the Word, Minister of the Sacraments, and Leader of the Community* (Congregation for the Clergy, 1999)—as well as documents that have originated since the Council from the bishops of the United States, such as *The Continuing Formation of Priests: Growing in Wisdom, Age, and Grace* (National Conference of Catholic Bishops [NCCB], 1984). NOCERCC has also provided valuable documents with a specific emphasis on the American context, such as the *Handbook for the Continuing Formation of Priests* (1994). At the same time, this plan is not simply a repetition of what is contained in previous documents. Rather, it seeks to focus the many elements contained in previous documents and apply them to the situation of priests in the United States at the beginning of a new century.

This plan of ongoing formation assumes the documents mentioned above. It also assumes the process of initial formation as described in the *Program of Priestly Formation* (PPF) (NCCB, fourth edition, 1992), which is the authoritative standard established by the U.S. bishops for seminaries in this country. This basic plan for the ongoing formation of priests elaborates chapter six of the *Program of Priestly Formation*, "The Continuing Formation of Priests" (nos. 549-572).

Finally, the basic plan of ongoing formation for priests assumes an authentic doctrinal understanding of the ministerial priesthood. At various points in the text, references and citations are provided that give indications of that doctrinal understanding, such as the doctrinal syntheses of Pope John Paul II found in *Pastores Dabo Vobis*. A more fully developed synthesis appears in the appendix to this document. There the reader can find a compact and clear doctrinal understanding of the ministerial priesthood as it appears in the *Program of Priestly Formation*, which represents the common doctrinal point of departure for both primary and ongoing formation.

The unifying thread for both parts of the plan is the grace and the task of *integration*, which fosters the living synthesis of priestly identity and priestly service. Integration is at the heart of ongoing formation, as priests grow in bringing together *who* they are and *what* they do. Their growth is really a growing integrity or connectedness of their ministry and their life. To use integration as a unifying focus of the plan simply follows the overall aim of Vatican II's *Decree on the Ministry and Life of Priests* (*Presbyterorum Ordinis*) (PO), which by the very deliberate phrasing of its title identified priestly ministry as shaping and giving rise to a new way of life. Similarly in *Pastores Dabo Vobis*, Pope John Paul II, speaking of the profound meaning of ongoing formation, affirms, "Ongoing formation helps the priest to *be* and *act* as a priest in the spirit and style of Jesus the Good Shepherd" (no. 73).

C. General Description: Ongoing Formation as the Integration of Priestly Identity and the Tasks of Priestly Ministry for the Sake of Mission

Programs, resources, and practices do not constitute ongoing formation. They are necessary instruments but always in service to the larger purpose and direction of formation. It is tempting, however, in an American context with its stress on practicality to identify formation with programs. Thus, it is important from the onset to identify the essence of ongoing formation.

Following the footsteps of Vatican II's *Presbyterorum Ordinis* and John Paul II's *Pastores Dabo Vobis*, we can define ongoing formation in this way: It is the continuing integration of priestly identity and functions or service for the sake of mission and communion with Christ and the Church. Each element of this definition bears careful examination.

To say that ongoing formation is "continuing" simply identifies it as a life-long task or process. That is why documents often speak of "permanent" formation. It truly is co-extensive with life itself. We never stop growing or being transformed.

For many, the word "integration" may be either vague or seem to reduce spirituality to psychological processes. In the context of ongoing formation, integration is quite specific and spiritual. It signals the movement toward a unity of life that draws together and dynamically relates who we are, what we do, and what we are about (our purpose or mission). As a movement toward a unity of life, the aim of integration is to find the *unum necessarium*, "the one necessary thing," of the Gospel and to live centered in it.

"Priestly identity" is something given sacramentally. It is also something consciously appropriated. In both dimensions, priestly identity shapes existence or the way of being in the world. It enables priests to say to themselves and to others who they are.

The "functions" of our lives are the tasks and operations that belong to us because of the responsibilities that have been given to us and that we have assumed. "Priestly functions" means the service that priests offer, the activities of their ministry.

Finally, "mission" names the purpose and direction given to priests that shapes and orders their commitments and responsibilities. The mission of priests is directly linked to the mission of the Church, which in turn depends entirely on the mission of Jesus Christ.

This brief examination of the particular components of the definition of ongoing formation can help us understand its importance and meaning. To identify ongoing formation as the continuing integration of priestly identity and function for the sake of mission and communion set us in a holistic context that touches many aspects of priestly ministry and life, which we will consider shortly in greater detail. Before that, in order to fill out the picture of ongoing formation itself, it helps to note some of the qualities or characteristics of ongoing formation for priests.

D. Essential Characteristics of Ongoing Formation

Ongoing formation follows the pattern of faith and God's action in its different dimensions. Ongoing formation is, first of all, *personal*. It belongs to individuals as their own responsibility to foster their own integration. At the same time, ongoing formation is *ecclesial* and *social*, and that is true in at least two ways. It unfolds in a context of the community of faith as well as the more defined community of the presbyterate with its bishop. Although formation has to do with an individual's growth, the community they serve—the Church—benefits greatly from the growth of its priests.

Ongoing formation begins with and is sustained by *commitments* made by priests and by the Church they serve. Without a deliberate or intentional decision to engage the process and without the willingness to support it, ongoing formation cannot happen. This means that the proper resources of time, personnel, and finances must be allotted.

Finally, although ongoing formation is essentially a process that unfolds in the ministry and life of priests, it does have a *programmatic* side. Planning, programs, various practices, and events serve as instruments, not to make formation happen, but to help it emerge in the course of ministry and life.

This preliminary sketch of ongoing formation allows us to examine the elements of identity, function/service, and mission in greater detail. Then, we can note the programs engaged by priests and supported by the Church that foster the process of integration of identity and function for the sake of mission.

E. Priestly Identity: Who I Am

Identity is constituted by everything that shapes our existence or way of being in the world and enables us to say who we are. Priests have a complex identity, which corresponds to the way they exist in the world. If they only filled a specific religious role in society, their identity would be quite simple. In fact, priests exist in the world in three principal ways that are interrelated. Priests exist as human beings. They also exist as believing Christians or disciples of Jesus Christ in his Church. Finally, they exist in a unique sacramental mode, as part of the order of presbyters in the Church.

The complexity of priestly identity gives rise to the differentiated programmatic dimensions of formation, designed to address the human, intellectual, pastoral, and spiritual aspects of priestly existence and identity. Later, we will consider these programmatic responses to the complex identity of priests. First we need to explore more deeply the different dimensions of priestly identity.

A GROWING, DEVELOPING HUMAN BEING

Priests are, first of all, human beings whose very humanity ought to be a bridge for communicating Jesus Christ to the world today (cf. PDV, no. 43). Their humanity reflects a complex make-up, the different dimensions of what it means to be human. Each dimension needs recognition and attention. Here we list the essential dimensions:

- *Physical*: Priests are embodied persons, whose living and functioning depend on the health and full functioning of their bodies.
- *Psychological*: The humanity of priests is especially prominent in their psychological capacities, which are cognitive, affective, and value-directed. The

cognitive capacity includes the ability to perceive or gather information, to understand, and to make judgments. The affective capacity includes the ability to feel and to connect with other human beings and the world through feeling. The value capacity includes the ability to cultivate attitudes that can direct commitments, actions, and patterns of behavior.

- *Sexual*: The sexuality of priests links both physical and psychological life. Sexuality represents a passion, an energy, and a direction for connecting, belonging, and giving life—in other words, for intimacy and generativity. Physical, psychological, and spiritual dimensions of life converge in human sexuality.
- *Cultural*: Priests in the United States exist in a cultural or, more accurately, a multicultural context. Culture provides the social tools for understanding the world, for shaping and working in it, and finally, for expressing its realties. In other words, culture provides a framework for exploring the human understanding of the world and acting in it—the stuff of science, technology, and the arts. In all of this, culture enables people to connect and collaborate with each other. Culture, however, is not only a tool that people use to shape the world, but the collective values and attitudes that shape people. It can be identified with the spirit of the age or the nation that continuously transmits cues for behavior, ideals to be pursued, and values to be cultivated. Culture, in this sense, can exercise a positive or negative influence in shaping life.
- *Social*: Priests live in a social order. They come from families, generally connect with some form of community, and are part of a larger society. Within society, they have a socially defined role. With other citizens or members of society, they are participants in political life through which people seek to live together peacefully and to prosper.

A BELIEVER IN AND DISCIPLE OF JESUS CHRIST

Priests are believing Christians and disciples of Jesus Christ. This is their grounding identity, the foundation upon which their specific sacramental presence and ministry in the Church as priests is built. First, they are baptized and profess their faith, and then they are sent to share in the apostolic mission.

The assumption is that they are not Christians or disciples merely in name. Rather, they have embarked on an intentional or deliberate spiritual journey. In this way, they are committed to a growing and transforming relationship with

14

their Lord by the power of the Holy Spirit, a relationship marked by the following dynamics:

- *Growing Faith*: A growing faith gives evidence of a growing relationship with a loving God and an insight into the revelation of God in Jesus Christ, accompanied by a greater practical wisdom of what that revelation means for living.
- *Growing Love*: Progress in the spiritual life has always been identified with a growth in *caritas*, the love of God, and linked to that, the love of others. Growing love or *caritas* is manifested in a progressive attachment to Jesus Christ, a greater willingness to share in his paschal mystery, a more authentic worship of God in spirit and truth, and an expanding and deepening compassion for others.
- *Growing Hope*: Hope in God enables us to trust in the promised future that God gives us. In the course of our earthly journey, growing hope is clear from the ever-more practical, direct, and generous ways that gospel values lead us to take action in the world to open a way for God's kingdom, God's future promise.

SHARING IN THE PRESBYTERAL ORDER

Through the sacrament of holy orders, through priestly ordination, priests not only assume new responsibilities and functions in the Church and world, they *exist* differently in and for the Church and the world. This different existence that gives rise to a specific identity has its sacramental foundation in a new relationship with Jesus Christ, a relationship that is lived out in a presbyterate and that, in the Western church, has become intimately connected to consecrated celibacy.

- *Being Conformed to Christ*: Through sacramental ordination priests are conformed to Jesus Christ, and this makes all the difference. In a single, compact paragraph in *Pastores Dabo Vobis*, John Paul II offers this synthesis:

> In the Church and on behalf of the Church, priests are a sacramental representation of Jesus Christ, the Head and Shepherd, authoritatively proclaiming his Word, repeating his acts of forgiveness and his offer of salvation, particularly in Baptism, Penance and the Eucharist, showing his loving concern to the point of a total gift of self for the flock, which they

gather into unity and lead to the Father through Christ and in the Spirit. In a word, priests exist and act in order to proclaim the Gospel to the world and to build up the Church in the name and person of Christ the Head and Shepherd." (no. 15)

The identity of priests is connected with their specific sacramental existence in relationship to Jesus Christ and the Church.

- *In a Presbyterate in Communion With its Bishop*: The sacramental relationship with Jesus Christ and the Church is not the individual possession of "the" priest. Priests exist as priests in a presbyterate gathered with its bishop. They draw their priestly identity as well from this presbyteral existence. John Paul II expresses it in this way: "By its very nature, the ordained ministry can be carried out only to the extent that the priest is united to Christ through sacramental participation in the priestly order, and thus to the extent that he is in hierarchical communion with his own Bishop. The ordained ministry has a radical *'communitarian form'* and can only be carried out as 'a collective work'" (PDV, no. 17).
- *In a Life of Chaste Celibacy*: In the Western church, priestly existence in relationship to Christ and to the Church has found expression in the discipline of chaste celibacy for her priests. Chaste celibacy is a way of being or existing as priest in relationship to Christ and the Church, and so it gives rise to a new identity. The christological and ecclesiological foundations for this practice (and implicitly the eschatological implications) are evident in this passage from *Pastores Dabo Vobis*: "The Church, as the Spouse of Jesus Christ, wishes to be loved by the priest in the total and exclusive manner in which Jesus Christ her Head and Spouse loved her. Priestly celibacy, then, is the gift of self *in* and *with* Christ *to* his Church and expresses the priest's service to the Church in and with the Lord" (no. 29).

F. Priestly Service or Ministry: What I Do

Ongoing formation for priests is the continuing integration of identity and function for the sake of mission. There is a vital connection between who priests are in virtue of their specific identity and what they do ministerially. We have examined priestly existence, which is human, Christian, and specifically sacramental. Then, it is important to identify another element in the process of integration—service or ministry, what priests do.

These men-disciples-priests, who hold this complex identity, also minister to or serve the community. There are many activities connected with their service. Generally, the Church has grouped them together in three categories: the ministry of word, the ministry of sacrament or sanctification, and the ministry of being pastor to the community of faith. Most recently, the Congregation for the Clergy has identified these dimensions of priestly service in the particular context of the new Christian millennium and the call for a new evangelization (*The Priest and the Third Christian Millennium: Teacher of the Word, Minister of the Sacraments, and Leader of the Community*, 1999).

MINISTRY OF THE WORD

Proclamation of the word of God is the *primum officium* or first task and responsibility of priests. The Second Vatican Council says, "For since nobody can be saved who has not first believed, it is the first task of priests as co-workers of the bishops to preach the Gospel of God to all" (PO, no 4).

The ministry of proclamation assumes a number of different forms. For example, it can be differentiated by the setting in which it takes place and its particular scope or purpose within that setting. Preaching, teaching, and counseling can all be examples of ministry of the word or proclamation. They do, however, reflect different methods and purposes, even if the ultimate goal is the communication of God's word to people.

Another way that the ministry of the word is differentiated is by the nature of its content. For example, kerygmatic or evangelical preaching aims to communicate the basic good news of Jesus Christ and call to faith those who have not heard it. Catechesis, on the other hand, forms those who already believe by deepening and expanding their understanding of faith. Homiletic preaching, which belongs specifically to the ordained, occurs in the context of sacramental celebrations and lets God's word prompt people to enter the celebration of the sacred mysteries in their lives. Parenesis is moral exhortation, especially as people face difficult or complex sets of moral choices. Prophetic preaching addresses the social situation in light of the demands of God's word. These are some of the principal ways in which the ministry of the word or proclamation is carried out.

MINISTRY OF THE SACRAMENTS

Priests celebrate and preside at the sacramental celebrations of the Church, preeminently the Eucharist. Furthermore, through the sacraments the faithful are able to participate in the transforming mysteries of Jesus Christ by the power of the Holy Spirit. So, in celebrating and presiding at the sacraments, priests carry on a ministry of sanctification.

In addition to celebrating and presiding at sacramental celebrations, priests are also responsible for directing the sacramental life of the Church. The sacraments are not limited simply to specific ritual moments. The sacraments initiate and lead people into a new way of living. Priests encourage the whole Church to *live* the sacraments, whether in the generous self-sacrificing love prompted by the Eucharist, or in living out compassionate forgiveness as a consequence of the sacrament of reconciliation, or in giving oneself entirely in loving and life-giving ways in the sacrament of marriage.

Finally, priests extend the sacramental celebration of the mysteries of Christ through their intercessory celebration of the Liturgy of the Hours for the sake of the whole body of Christ.

GIVING A SHEPHERD'S CARE TO THE COMMUNITY OF FAITH

Priests are conformed to Jesus Christ, the Good Shepherd; they continue to care for the flock entrusted to them in various ways. Obviously, the initial formation of communities of faith and then sustaining them on their journey is a pastoral task of fundamental importance. At the same time, individual communities, especially parishes, do not stand alone. Priests need to stand for and nurture the bonds that link the local community with the diocese and the universal Church. At times, priests shepherd a community by encouraging and fostering its discernment of God's direction and, at appropriate times, by giving direction. For many American priests, the context of their pastoral work is a culture different than their native one, a situation that calls for great flexibility of spirit. In general, a shepherd's care for a community of faith means presiding over it, moderating it, and, when necessary, representing it.

Ongoing formation is the continuing integration of priests' identity and ministry for the sake of mission. We have noted the principal elements of identity and service or ministry. What remains is to consider the mission.

G. Priestly Mission: For What Purpose

The purpose of priestly ministry, as church documents abundantly indicate, is to serve the Church. The Church exists in different ways as a parish, as a diocese, and as the universal Church. Ultimately, the Church itself continues the mission of Jesus Christ in the world. It does so as mystery, communion, and mission. The Church that priests serve is a mystery, a great sacrament of God's design for humanity, for ultimate unity in God. The Church is also communion. As communion, the Church is a sign of peace and an instrument of reconciliation in the world, even now a partial but real participation in the very life of the Trinity (cf. *Pastoral Constitution on the Church in the Modern World* [*Gaudium et Spes*] [GS], no. 24). Finally, the Church that priests serve is itself in mission. For it is an evangelized and evangelizing community that seeks to extend the mission, message, and person of Jesus Christ to the world.

The mission of the Church points beyond itself. It rests in Jesus Christ, and it looks to a future destiny. Priests serve the mission of the Church to the extent that they sustain and encourage the Church to stay on course in its mission and on its journey as the pilgrim people of God, until they arrive at their destination and consummation by sharing fully in the mystery of God. At that time, the mission will be completed, and the earthly Church will be completely transformed into the heavenly Church.

H. The Context for Ongoing Formation for Priests in the United States at the Beginning of the Twenty-First Century

Before considering practical implications of ongoing formation for priests by translating principles and values into programs, it is crucial to note the context of ongoing formation in the United States at the beginning of a new century. Context not only shapes programs and practical possibilities, it also tells us that the task of ongoing formation for priests is very urgent, that it requires immediate and significant attention. Context links ongoing formation with the larger life of the Church and the world.

There are at least ten significant contexts for the ongoing formation of priests. Each context invites much fuller development. For our purposes, it is enough to note the context and add a brief explanation.

1. *Realization of the Need for Ongoing Personal and Professional Development*: As all sectors in society have paid more attention to the need for ongoing professional development, so, too, priests have taken advantage of a variety of opportunities to enhance such ongoing personal and professional formation. In some instances, a too narrow concept of priestly ordination as capping years of seminary preparation, rather than as a beginning of a life of ever-expanding priestly service, has impeded this necessary journey of growth.

2. *Divisions in Presbyterates*: Presbyterates find themselves divided along a number of lines, such as age, theological perspectives, formational background—whether native-born or foreign-born—and ministerial focus. There is great urgency in developing presbyteral unity, something we will consider in greater detail later, because it belongs to the prayer of Jesus "that they may all be one . . . that the world may believe" (Jn 17:21). Presbyteral unity is instrumental in bringing faith to the world. Ongoing formation brings priests together not simply to rally around a common task but to proceed in faith with the mission of unity. Ongoing formation serves the unity of presbyterates especially by regrounding priests in their common faith vision and by offering them a common vocabulary of communication.

3. *Diminishing Numbers of Priests, More Complex Circumstances for Priestly Service*: The lessened numbers of priests is a documented fact of life. That may change for the better or the worse. The fact remains that this is our reality now. It is not, however, simply a matter of fewer priests. It is also the fact of far more complicated circumstances in the Church in the United States. Complications stem in part from the happy circumstance of increasing numbers of Catholics. Some of that increase stems from immigration, especially of those who speak Spanish. Catholics in the United States have arrived in many ways. Some find themselves affluent, well educated, and comfortable. In large numbers, other Catholics are quite poor, marginalized, and even oppressed in our social structures. Some Catholics have great voice in the direction of this nation, while others are unheard. The combination of fewer numbers of priests with ever more complex

circumstances of the Church in the United States presses the urgency of ongoing formation of priests. Formation can be a vehicle to understand and address the complexity and, at the same time, be a means to cultivate a necessary apostolic flexibility among priests.

4. *The Counterpoint of Current Cultural Sexual Mores, Values, and the Commitments of Priests*: There is a dramatic contrast between the current American cultural climate of sexuality and the standards and values of the Church, especially as these are embodied in priests' celibate commitment. In a previous age, priests might expect the culture not to understand their celibate commitment but to respect it—perhaps, at times, even to admire it. Today the former social support for celibacy is gone. Highly publicized cases of priests' sexual misconduct have cast a shadow of incredibility on the professed values enshrined in the celibate commitment. All this suggests an urgent need for ongoing formation that enables priests to interiorize their commitment at a deep level and learn how to live with less cultural support than existed in the past.

5. *International Priests and Multiculturalism in the United States*: We are a nation of immigrants, and foreign-born priests have been a part of the landscape of the Church in the United States for generations. There seems to be, however, a growing dependence on international priests precisely at a time when Catholicism is solidly established in American life. Similarly, even priests born in the United States find themselves compelled by pastoral necessity to learn a foreign language, especially Spanish, to serve the people under their care. The integration of international priests and the welcome of new Catholic immigrants underscores the need for ongoing formation for priests, who must come to terms with each other and with recently arrived populations in a new way.

6. *Social Shifts and Realignment of Church Resources*: In the last twenty-five years the United States has been marked by notable shifts in the economy, moving, for example, from a manufacturing-based economy to one driven by information technology. Demographic shifts have taken place and continue to do so in the major cities. Rural areas have also experienced major transitions. All this represents a remarkable quantity of social change, and it has had implications for the organization of the Church's mission. The closure of parishes, for example, has been an extraordinarily painful experience for many dioceses and priests. The future seems to hold more social change in store and, with it, a need for more realignment of church

resources. This immensely complicated and delicate task will summon all the talents, wisdom, and spiritual patience that priests have to offer. Again, ongoing formation seems essential to meet future challenges.

7.   *Social Engagement of the Church in Matters of Justice, Life, and Reconciliation*: The Catholic Church in the United States has a voice and a responsibility to speak on behalf of justice issues, life issues, and national reconciliation. The American tendency to privatize religion and to separate it, at least implicitly, from public life creates some resistance to hearing the voice of the Church. There are Catholics as well who are convinced that the Church should stay out of public discourse on social matters. In fact, the enormous weight of these issues and the call to be faithful to prophetic witness underscore the urgency of ongoing formation for priests who must exercise leadership.

8.   *The New Evangelization*: Pope John Paul II has set a pace for the Church entering a new millennium. He has called for a new evangelization, primarily targeted at reclaiming those who are Catholic Christian in name but weakly or loosely connected with faith and Church in fact. In an American context, sociologists have documented that large segments of our population, including our Catholic population, are attracted to the spiritual journey but reluctant to establish ties with institutional religion. The challenge facing the Church and, particularly, its priests is to link the spiritual quest of people with the faith traditions of the Catholic community of faith. This integral approach to a new evangelization in the United States demands a clarity of theological vision and a depth of spiritual commitment that priests can only summon in themselves if they are studying and praying well, if they are engaged in ongoing formation.

9.   *Fluidity and Polarization in the Post-Vatican II Church*: The process of conciliar renewal is short by historical standards and seemingly incomplete. In the United States, the years after the Council until now have been marked by a certain fluidity in liturgical practice, catechesis, and ecclesial organization. This indeterminateness seems to have generated vocal reactions in church life that want either the restoration of a pre-Vatican II Church or the complete dismantling of the Church and its re-assembly as an entirely new reality. The majority of Catholics seem to identify themselves with a quiet, faithful middle ground. The concern for a deeper assimilation of the renewal called for by the Council, however, will remain for the foreseeable future. Renewal will require leadership, much of which must come from

priests, that is theologically formed and spiritually sustained. This prospect highlights the need for ongoing formation.

10. *Sharing Many Ministries and Retrieving the Core of Priestly Identity*: As the *Catechism of the Catholic Church* indicates "the laity can also feel called, or be in fact called, to cooperate with their pastors in the service of the ecclesial community, for the sake of its growth and life. This can be done through the exercise of different kinds of ministries according to the grace and charisms which the Lord has been pleased to bestow on them (no. 910). These many kinds of ministries have been a blessing for the postconciliar Church. At the same time, priests retain a unique and irreplaceable identity and function in the Church, even as many others who are not ordained assume responsibilities in and for the Church in the world. If this expansion of ministry is to develop authentically, priests will need to contribute to it with their leadership, encouragement, and expertise. At the same time, they must be sufficiently secure in their own identity, so that new ecclesial developments do not pose a threat to them. If priests are to contribute to the encouragement of ministries in the Church and retain a secure sense of themselves, they will depend in great measure on the mechanisms of ongoing formation. Especially to be valued will be the development of skills of collaboration with growing parish staffs and the skills of consensus building in working with parish groups, such as pastoral councils.

This consideration of the context from ten perspectives enables us now to examine more directly the shape of ongoing formation for priests, some of the practical implications of the values and convictions of which we have identified.

I. The Programs, Resources, and Practices to Foster Ongoing Formation

Programs, resources, and practices, we noted, do not constitute ongoing formation. They do not make it happen, nor does their employment offer the assurance that it is, indeed, taking place. They are, however, necessary means or instruments to foster ongoing formation. The following section will explain how programs, resources, and practices can be organized to serve their purpose of fostering ongoing formation.

The programs must hold fast to the understanding of ongoing formation as the continuing integration of identity and function for the sake of mission and communion with Christ and the Church, the growing and vital connection of who priests are and what they do for the sake of the mission.

Different life stages, we already noted, mean that the task of integration will also be different, and this fact obviously has implications for programs and resources. There is formation that is specific to newly ordained priests, recently ordained priests, priests preparing for the first pastorate, middle-aged priests, priests preparing for retirement, and retired priests. Each group has its specific program needs. Still, there are core pieces of identity and service that are constant across priests' lifetimes no matter their age or the particular circumstances of their ministry. A part of formation truly does remain ongoing, permanent, or constant. That steady core forms the substance of the program and resource descriptions that follow. Programs specific to age and circumstance are considered in part two of the basic plan.

Finally, *Pastores Dabo Vobis* divides ongoing priestly formation into four categories: human, intellectual, pastoral, and spiritual. Although programs may overlap categories, it seems best to retain the distinct categories proposed in the apostolic exhortation.

J. Human Formation

Human formation ought to have as its aim the fuller development of priests' humanity so that their humanity can be a "bridge" for communicating Jesus Christ to men and women today (cf. PDV, no. 43). In this context, *Pastores Dabo Vobis* speaks of priests' relational capacities: "Of special importance is the capacity to relate to others. This is truly fundamental for a person who is called to be responsible for a community and to be a 'man of communion'" (no. 43).

If human formation aims to cultivate the humanity of priests so that their humanity is instrumental in communicating Jesus Christ and that they can be authentic "men of communion," then the general means of such formation are clear. Psychological and sociological self-knowledge, for example, are essential. Cultivating one's capacity for communication as listener and speaker strengthens the capacity for dialogue and communion. Attention ought to be given to any personality quirks that impede communion. In addition, cultivating one's capacity for communion also includes regularly scheduled time for rest and vacation.

Cultivation of our humanity cannot ignore the body. Our embodiment means the need to care for our physical well-being, not only maintaining health but training the body to sustain an active and invested life. An essential element of the priest's embodiment is his sexuality. Ongoing formation necessarily includes an increasing integration of one's sexuality. As noted previously, sexuality is an energy or passion directed toward connecting, belonging, and giving life. While a celibate commitment is not expressed in genital sexual activity or in an exclusive intimate relationship, the priest remains a sexual person who is expected to develop mature expressions of chaste love and caring. As the priest internalizes his celibate commitment, his sexuality is ever more directed toward a vibrant spiritual life, nurturing appropriate friendships in a passionate, caring priestly ministry. The human integration of affectivity is manifest in appropriate responses to the thwarting of basic needs and the experiences of significant loss. Without affective integration, these situations give rise either to debilitating depression or destructive anger. Human formation seeks to foster affective integration.

Finally, human formation entails contact with the culture: the arts, sciences, and politics of human life. These studies and involvements keep priests in touch with their own lives and the lives of those whom they serve.

These are the general means of human formation. The specific means include events, resources, and programs. For example, human formation, as we have described it, can sometimes occur through a one-to-one dialogue of friendship. At times, professional counseling can appropriately and effectively address human growth issues for priests. It need not be reserved, as unfortunately it is in the perceptions of some, for the treating of illness. Professionally facilitated groups that focus on interpersonal dynamics can be effective instruments of human formation. Similarly, human formation can happen in the context of feedback, when individuals are helped to see and appreciate their impact in various situations, so that they can learn from that knowledge and confirm what is good and change what is less opportune. Programs of periodic review and assessment are useful feedback mechanisms.

As we have described it, human formation has a direct, personal, and experiential dimension. Study can also foster human formation for priests. An intellectual component in human formation enables priests to understand themselves and others better. Certain courses, seminars, workshops, or directed readings could advance the human formation of priests. The following themes and fields of study serve as a sample of this approach:

- The human life cycle (psychology)
- Gender differences and communication (anthropology)
- A profile of the United States or the local population (sociology)
- Unexamined assumptions of contemporary life (philosophy)
- Expressions of human experience in literature, art, drama, and film (fine arts)
- Science that shapes our life (science)
- Diversity and democracy in the United States (political science)
- Information technology (computer science)

K. Intellectual Formation

Intellectual formation aims to deepen the understanding of faith. It seeks to link theoretical knowledge with a practical wisdom, so that priests can serve their people more effectively. This kind of intellectual formation is not classroom bound nor does it result in detached speculation. It truly is faith seeking understanding, driven forward by love for the people served. The fathers of the Church are models for this kind of formation. They were pastors who were theologians, and they were theologians thoroughly immersed in pastoral life.

Two areas of intellectual formation require special attention:

1. *The Faith Convictions That Ground Priests' Mission and Ministry*: Throughout the course of their priestly ministry, priests must revisit and study what they are doing, how they are representing Christ, and why. If priestly ministry is not merely the exercise of professional expertise but a true service in faith for God's people, then priests must continually ground their ministry and life in the underlying assumptions of faith. This is not done once and for all. This is a fundamental and often repeated retrieval and reflection on the faith foundations of priestly ministry. Regularly, priests must return to their

roots in the Church, in the mystery of Christ, ultimately, in the very mystery of trinitarian life. Like their brothers and sisters in faith, priests are pilgrims and struggling disciples. They need to return regularly and deliberately to the holy mysteries that ground their ministry and life.

How do priests revisit this holy memory to re-ground and re-orient themselves in ministry? Are there programs or structures available to do this? Some suggest themselves immediately. The annual event of priests gathered with their bishop at the Chrism Mass is a particular moment for such retrieval. The diocesan celebrations of priests' ordinations, anniversaries, and deaths can be another. Days of renewal, such as the days of sanctification encouraged by the Holy See, are an occasion for returning to the sources in faith for ministry and mission. The annual diocesan retreat can be another occasion. An especially powerful tool of faith retrieval and re-grounding is found in small groups of priests gathered to reflect not on what they do or how they do it but on the holy origin of their ministry.

2. *Updating in Major Theological Areas of Special Pastoral Concern*: The seminary program is limited in its time frame. It also suffers from the seminarians' lack of experience. Furthermore, seminaries cannot fully anticipate developments in theology or new challenges in pastoral situations. For this reason, theological updating or *aggiornamento* is a continuing and pressing need of intellectual formation throughout the course of priestly ministry. Some examples of special areas of pastoral concern that require an authentic pastoral theology and theological reflection on specific situations in the lives of our people, parishes, and society (PDV, no. 57; PPF, nos. 341, 398) include the following:

- Revelation-faith and the relationship to reason
- Ecumenism and inter-faith dialogue, especially in the context of the United States
- The authority of the Bible and its relevance for daily life
- Sacramental theology
- Theology of priesthood
- Theology of marriage
- Theology of suffering, illness, and death
- Sin in a personal and social context
- Medical-moral issues
- Questions of justice and the Church's social teaching

The processes and programs for intellectual formation need careful examination. A lecture format, although occasionally useful, is a very limited form of adult learning, especially for practitioners, as priests in parochial ministry are. Dioceses have often focused on bringing in a speaker for workshops, convocations, and study days. Theological updating can be accomplished in other formats and, often, more effectively. Videos, the internet, guided self study, and peer learning in small groups not only offer more flexibility in the study process but they also respect the lived experience of the priests.

L. Pastoral Formation

Pastoral formation entails the development of skills and competencies that enable priests to serve their people well. Pastoral formation is not divorced from intellectual or theological education. It is, however, the more practical side of theology. "As pastors of the People of God in America, priests must also be alert to the challenges of the world today and sensitive to the problems and hopes of their people, sharing their experiences and growing, above all, in solidarity towards the poor. They should be careful to discern the charisms and strengths of the faithful who might be leaders in the community, listening to them and through dialogue encouraging their participation and co-responsibility" (EA, no. 39).

Competencies and skills by their very nature are acquired and developed through instruction, application, and practice. Attempts to develop certain critical pastoral competencies and skills for priestly ministry will meet with limited success in the course of a seminary program. The real opportunity to learn and cultivate such pastoral competencies and skills is after ordination, when the opportunity for application and practice becomes available.

Certain competencies and skills emerge directly from priests' identity and what service they are called to render for the community. Other competencies and skills are shaped by the particular needs of our American culture and the historical moment. Among those competencies and skills that perennially belong to priests are the following:

- Preaching and proclaiming the word
- Celebrating and presiding at the sacraments
- Leading prayer
- Performing pastoral counseling and spiritual direction
- Directing the catechesis of adults and children

Particular features of our American culture and historical moment encourage priests to develop these competencies and skills:

- Social analysis and community organization
- Cross-cultural communication
- Foreign language skills
- The initiation, direction, and supervision of the various pastoral efforts of the Church

The Church that priests serve is both a spiritual and a visible-institutional reality. Part of their continuing pastoral formation must include knowledge of the ways of *institutional leadership* and *management*. In their pastoral function, priests are responsible for the Church as a community ordered in love. Additionally, they function as employers and as stewards of the temporal goods of the Church. None of these responsibilities is outside the pale of their pastoral task. All dimensions of management require thoughtful attention, specific knowledge, and particular competencies and skills to make appropriate applications of the knowledge to practical situations. Even as more and more pastors hire business managers to be directly responsible for temporal matters, priests still need some management development.

Ongoing pastoral formation ought to include the following areas:

- Canon law updates
- Personnel management
- Conflict resolution
- Financial management
- Effective leadership in meetings
- Facilitation of parish communication

M. Spiritual Formation

Spiritual formation is a life-long task that priests share with other followers of Jesus Christ. Its aim is for priests to become better disciples of Jesus Christ and, specifically, to become more transparent sacramental signs of him in whose person and name they act.

The ongoing spiritual formation of priests needs to move in five dimensions: formation in discipleship, formation in pastoral charity, formation in celibacy, formation in obedience, and formation in simplicity of lifestyle. The benefit of the guidance and wisdom of spiritual directors and confessors can be of enormous assistance to priests in their ongoing spiritual formation.

FORMATION IN DISCIPLESHIP

Pastores Dabo Vobis follows Vatican II's *Decree on the Training of Priests* (*Optatam Totius*) in identifying spiritual formation as learning "to live in holy, familiar and attentive union with the Father, through his Son Jesus Christ in the holy Spirit" (no. 8). Furthermore, spiritual formation means drawing close to Jesus Christ as friend in every detail of life (cf. PDV, no. 45). As spiritual writers have consistently noted, the life of discipleship is a shedding of illusions and the embrace of real or authentic self in Christ.

The means for nurturing such formation in discipleship include a daily life of prayer that includes contact with the word of God along with the cultivation of a contemplative attitude and faithful participation in the sacramental life of the Church, especially the Eucharist and the sacrament of reconciliation. Priests' discipleship also finds expression and growth through their daily celebration of the Liturgy of the Hours, which as the prayer of the Church links them with the whole body of Christ in praise, petition, and thanksgiving. Discipleship also entails a daily taking up of one's cross through a process of self-denial, self-discipline, detachment, and an embracing of the circumstances of one's life as providentially given by God. The cultivation of a devotional life, which can include, for example, the rosary, the stations of the cross, and visits to the Blessed Sacrament, fosters discipleship by keeping believers in contact with Mary, the Mother of the Lord, and the saints, the friends of God. Discipleship is also fostered by nourishing the affective dimension of priests' faith journey.

FORMATION IN PASTORAL CHARITY

In addition to the journey of discipleship that priests share with other believers, they also traverse a spiritual path marked by their specific identity as priests and the specific priestly service they render to the Church and the world. *Presbyterorum Ordinis* of Vatican II envisions the spiritual integration of priests' ministry and lives, their unity of life, in *pastoral charity*: "Priests will unify their lives by uniting themselves with Christ in recognition of the Father's will and in the gift of themselves to the flock entrusted to them. In this way, by adopting the role of the good shepherd they will find in the practice of pastoral charity itself the bond of priestly perfection which will harmonize their lives and activity" (no. 14). In other words, as priests give themselves to their people in proclaiming the word, celebrating the sacraments, leading prayer, interceding for the community, and leading the community, they will find their unity of life, their spiritual formation in the unifying love of Christ, the Good Shepherd, who gave his very life for us.

There are specific means whereby this unifying and integrating pastoral love becomes more conscious and more accessible to priests. Spiritual direction, for example, is an extraordinarily useful means for retrieving the experience of ministry, the presence of the Lord, and the integrating-unifying directions that God gives through the ministry. In presbyteral fraternity, priests can come to terms with the unifying love of Christ the Good Shepherd as the source and goal of their ministry and lives. That presbyteral fraternity takes various forms: the presbyterate with its bishop, priests' support or prayer groups, priests' friendships with one another that pursue their deep common bond in Christ, and various forms of mentoring that occur in a presbyterate. Retreats and days of renewal can also be integrating moments. Forms of spiritual associations, such as third orders, secular institutes, and pious unions, can offer possibilities for appropriating and deepening unity of life in Christ and spiritual formation. Sabbaticals can be seasons of grace that allow for a deeper sense of spiritual formation. Spiritual reading can serve a similar purpose.

FORMATION IN CELIBACY

The spiritual formation of priests is shaped decisively by their celibate commitment. The seminary offers formation *for* celibacy—a vision, a challenge, and a set of practical possibilities for making and living one's celibate commitment as a priest. Even the very best seminary program cannot prepare priests for a lifetime of celibate living in the context of priestly ministry. In addition to formation *for* celibacy, there needs to be formation *in* celibacy, for those already ordained and living out their commitment and facing questions, challenges, and graced possibilities.

Formation in celibacy is not simply focused on living with the renunciation of marriage. Formation in celibacy necessarily includes a direct and honest facing of one's sexuality and an ever-increasing freedom in expressing one's sexuality within an appropriate celibate context. Its overall aim centers on deepening the experiences of solitude, communion, love, and giving life. The motivation for the celibate commitment is pastoral charity, the all-encompassing love of Christ, the Good Shepherd for his people, as we noted above. Practically, formation in celibacy revisits three essential elements: the rationale for celibacy, the skills needed for celibate living, and the supportive resources to sustain the commitment and the life.

The *rationale* for celibacy needs to be revisited regularly. In other words, priests need to re-appropriate the spiritual sense of celibacy in light of their lived experience. Just as husband and wife cannot take each other for granted but need to reappropriate their love for each other in deliberate and conscious ways, so too priests must reclaim the sense of their celibacy as an act of love for God and God's people in the Church.

Priests also need to keep learning and refining the *skills* for celibate living. These are the human, interpersonal, and spiritual strategies for healthy and generative loving and living.

Finally, priests need the *supportive resources*—personal, ecclesial, and social—to sustain and nourish them in their celibate commitment. These may include a genuine sense of fraternity in the presbyterate, a healthy relationship with one's family of origin, priest support groups, and honest friendships.

Without a reason for celibacy, without the skills or means to live it out, and without a supportive and encouraging context, significant difficulties are bound to arise. With a reason, with means, and with support, celibacy is not only tolerable but indeed a fulfilling path of loving God and others and bringing new life to the world. Clearly, although celibacy fits best under "spiritual formation"—its true horizon—many other areas of priests' formation converge in it: human, psychological, physical, and ministerial.

In remembering and developing a rationale for celibacy, bishops—as well as senior clergy whose wisdom is invaluable for the whole presbyterate—play an important role. The skills of celibate living can be studied and prayed over in workshops, spiritual direction, retreats, counseling, and the mutual mentoring that can happen in priest groups. Supportive resources for celibacy ought to be found in the presbyterate gathered with the bishop and among the laity.

FORMATION IN OBEDIENCE

Obedience for priests, especially diocesan priests, is an apostolic obedience. The Second Vatican Council identified the apostolic dimension of priestly obedience in *Presbyterorum Ordinis*: "Priestly obedience, inspired through and through by the spirit of co-operation, is based on that sharing of the episcopal ministry which is conferred on priests by the sacrament of order and the canonical mission" (no. 7).

The *Directory on the Ministry and Life of Priests* cites canon law as well as the Second Vatican Council in specifying priestly obedience: "Priests have a 'special obligation to show reverence and obedience to the Supreme Pontiff and to their own Ordinary.' In virtue of his belonging to a determined presbyterate, the priest is charged with the service of a particular Church, in which the principle and foundation of unity is the Bishop. . ." (no. 62).

Priests' obedience has a christological foundation. The word made flesh came among us in obedience to the Father's will. His holy mission continues through his Church, which is hierarchically structured and whose very structure for the sake of mission requires obedience.

Priests not only make a promise of obedience at the time of ordination, they are also invited to grow in obedience, so that the Church's mission may advance through healthy collaboration and greater fidelity to God's will and design.

The process of growing obedience implies a real relationship between priests and their bishop, one that is marked by honest and direct communication. Growing obedience also means reading the signs of the times in union with the bishop and presbyterate to identify God's call in a given situation or set of circumstances. Finally, growing obedience means the practice of regular prayerful submission to what is asked.

FORMATION IN SIMPLICITY OF LIFE

Presbyterorum Ordinis says that a right attitude toward the goods of this world is essential for priests, because his mission "like that of the Church is carried out in the middle of the world and . . . created goods are necessary for the personal development of man" (no. 67).

In the measure that they approach the world with gratitude, simplicity, and generosity, priests grow in authentic sense of the world's goods. These attitudes and elements of lifestyle are rooted in Jesus Christ.

God pronounced an original blessing over the world at its creation. That blessing reached its perfect fulfillment in the incarnation, the mystery of the word made flesh. Jesus, although rich, emptied himself and made himself poor, so that we might become rich (cf. Phil 2:6-11; 2 Cor 8:9). As he went about his public ministry, he did so completely unencumbered: "Foxes have dens and birds of the sky have nests, but the Son of Man has nowhere to rest his head" (Lk 9:58). Finally, on the cross Jesus gives himself completely to the Father for our sake. In Jesus Christ priests see the pattern and the possibilities for their own relationship to the world and the things of the world: gratitude, simplicity, and generosity.

Priests grow in the right use of this world's goods by embracing a way of life based on the principles of Catholic stewardship. Indeed, such an attitude will give the priest frequent opportunities to express prayerful gratitude for God's many blessings. They also grow by taking responsibility for the material dimension of their lives, for example, through saving and planning wisely for their ministerial needs and their personal future.

Priests grow in a simplicity of lifestyle through a regular and prayerful scrutiny of their lives that identifies whatever would encumber them in their ministry and then eliminating it. Finally, simplicity and a spirit of poverty are always linked in the Gospels with generosity. Priests grow spiritually by the practiced use and distribution of their material resources for others, especially the poor.

THE STUDY OF SPIRITUALITY

The emphasis in spiritual formation is on the practice of spirituality, the cultivation of our experience of God by the power of the Holy Spirit. Walking in the footsteps of St. Teresa of Jesus, we can also say that it is a matter both of experience and knowledge. Fundamentally, it is something lived, but it is also something studied.

For priests, the study of spirituality includes topics and areas that can serve to nourish their spiritual life and, at the same time, enable them to be more available instruments for the spiritual growth of their people. Some significant themes and topics for priests to pursue in their ongoing spiritual formation are the following:

- Spirituality in a specifically Catholic Christian context
- Spiritual resources and practices from the tradition, specifically for priests
- Spiritual classics as a resource for ministry and life
- The spiritual life cycle of priests and others
- The art of learning about spirituality from various traditions
- Priests as intercessors and teachers of prayer
- Priestly spirituality as ministerial and integrative
- The meaning of ongoing conversion of life
- The spirituality of celibate life

N. The Responsibility for the Ongoing Formation of Priests

Earlier sections of this plan have identified the nature and urgency of ongoing formation for priests as well as some of the practical possibilities for translating values and convictions into programs and resources. In the end, if ongoing formation is to take place, someone must be responsible for it. We have considered the what, why, and how of ongoing formation for priests. What remains is the who.

INDIVIDUAL PRIESTS

Individual priests are responsible for their ongoing formation. Their responsibility is linked to their commitment at ordination to serve well the people of

God through their ministry and through their own personal faith commitment. Priests in dialogue with their bishop, his representative, or other members of the presbyterate need to map out their plan of ongoing formation.

At the same time, it seems possible, in light of everything that has been said, to determine a basic minimum. For example, as a basic minimum for formation the following elements would need to be in place:

- Fifty-two contact hours of education per year (in other words, one hour per week)
- One week of retreat
- Daily prayer (especially the celebration of the Eucharist and the Liturgy of the Hours)
- Monthly celebration of the sacrament of reconciliation, perhaps in conjunction with spiritual direction
- Monthly contact with a priest group or its equivalent

BISHOPS AND THEIR DELEGATES

Bishops have responsibility for the ongoing formation of priests. That is abundantly clear in conciliar and postconciliar documents. Surely, the first way they exercise that responsibility is by providing the personal example of their own commitment to ongoing formation. Other dimensions of that responsibility are not spelled out. It may be helpful, then, to identify in what way the bishop is directly responsible for ongoing formation and in what way he ought to make provisions for the ongoing formation of priests of the diocese.

1. *Bishop's Direct Responsibility*:
- The receipt of a regular report from those charged with the ongoing formation of priests on the "state of soul" of the presbyterate and any particular concerns
- At least three contact points with the presbyterate at large, e.g., Chrism Mass, a study day, or a diocesan retreat (as well as the presbyteral convocation when it is held)
- A periodic conversation held either directly or through the bishop's delegate with each priest concerning his ongoing formation to provide for accountability and encouragement

2. *Bishop's Provision for Ongoing Formation*:

- Provides for the adequate staffing of an office for the ongoing formation of priests (bishop functions as the guarantor of encouragement, time, and resources)
- Appoints a director to organize, ensure funding for, and communicate the resources of human, intellectual, pastoral, and spiritual formation (whether diocesan based or drawn from other institutions)
- Appoints and oversees a committee of priests (perhaps drawn from the presbyteral council) and others to regularly examine the process of ongoing formation in its various dimensions
- Supervises the director to establish linkage between the ongoing formation of priests and other diocesan efforts, e.g., evangelization, catechesis, worship, justice and peace, and lay formation
- Through the mechanisms of diocesan communication, communicates the values, purposes, and activities of the ongoing formation of priests to the people of God

O. Accountability

The best-laid plans for ongoing formation will amount to very little if they are not accompanied by a spirit and structure of accountability. Priests are answerable to the Church, to their people, and to themselves and their own sense of integrity, as they grow in their humanity, discipleship, and priestly ministry.

The word "accountability" in the context of ministry may be relatively new. The reality, however, stems from New Testament traditions. Paul, for example, especially in 2 Corinthians makes himself accountable to God, the church community, and himself. The following passage gives an example of how he stands accountable for a particular ministerial-apostolic decision: "But I call upon God as witness, on my life, that it is to spare you that I have not yet gone to Corinth. Not that we lord it over your faith; rather, we work together for your joy, for you stand firm in the faith. For I decided not to come to you again in painful circumstances. For if I inflict pain upon you, then who is there to cheer me except the one pained by me? And I wrote as I did so that when I came I might not be pained by those in whom I should have rejoiced, confident about all of you that my joy is that of all of you" (2 Cor 1:23-24; 2:1-3).

The Church, especially through the bishop and other presbyters, has a right to call priests to accountability for the ways that they have or have not fostered their human, intellectual, pastoral, and spiritual growth. Priests ought also to make themselves accountable for their ongoing formation. A simple way to do this is by sharing their choices and commitments for ongoing formation with their staff and people. They let their local community know, "This is what I am doing to serve you better." Sharing formational commitments with a spiritual director, friends, and priest support groups also facilitates a sense of accountability. A public position renders priests more visibly accountable for following through on a commitment to grow as men, disciples, and priests.

Part Two

FORMATION AT DIFFERENT AGES

A. A Good Beginning: Ongoing Formation in the First Years of Priesthood

INTRODUCTION

The first five years of ordained ministry are very important. They set a pace for the years that stretch ahead. They also lay a foundation for the future and provide a point of reference across a lifetime of priestly ministry.

Many events, as we shall shortly see, mark the first years of priesthood. All of them fit into a single frame of transition, the transition of newly ordained priests from the major seminary into their first parochial assignment. In an initial and decisive way, newly ordained priests embark on a formational journey of integration as they seek to link who they are and what they do, their priestly identity and service. They make themselves available to God's transforming power at work in their ministry and lives.

The following section will consider the ongoing formation of newly ordained priests in four steps: (1) a detailed description of the event of transition for the newly ordained; (2) an identification of the principal tasks and challenges that the newly ordained face; (3) a naming of their spiritual concerns viewed through the themes of temptation, grace, and discernment; (4) and finally, a consideration of programmatic responses to the needs of transition into priestly ministry.

EVENT

The general frame of transition from the major seminary to the first parochial assignment contains many events and experiences. Some have to do with departure, others with arrival, and still others with inner movements.

Departure from the seminary is usually a highly anticipated moment and a greatly welcomed one when it finally arrives. It does, however, signal a significant leave-taking. Newly ordained leave the seminary and, at the same time, leave behind a familiar setting that has been the context of their lives for at least four years. They also leave behind important relationships that may continue but in an altered way because of patterns that marked their lives during the time of preparation.

Priestly ordination signals another departure from student status, the state of being "in preparation for," to the status of a recognized and activated worker or minister of the Gospel. At this point, newly ordained are also conscious of leaving a way of living their Christian vocation among Christ's faithful people (*The Vocation and the Mission of the Lay Faithful in the Church and in the World* [*Christifideles Laici*] [CL]) to assume a new position and responsibility among and for that holy people.

Arrivals also become important. The newly ordained arrive in a new community and settle into new living arrangements. They arrive in the midst of a new set of established co-workers. They arrive in a new community with a new position or role as priest. They arrive into a new set of daily tasks.

Finally, the event of transition into priestly ministry contains inner experiences, which we will consider in more detail shortly. Ordination establishes priests in a new way of being in and for the Church by configuring them to Jesus Christ, Head and Shepherd. And even though this new identity is conferred in ordination, it may not be fully and consciously appropriated for some time. Another inner experience is a significant shift of focus from the development and formation of oneself during the years of preparation to a centering in service and mission to others as an ordained priest.

These are some of the pieces that form the event of transition for newly ordained. They leave, they arrive, they sense inner movements. It is no small matter. Were one to compare this transition into priestly ministry to other kinds of human experience, it might be like leaving home, graduating from school, beginning a career, getting married, and starting a family—but all at once.

TASKS AND CHALLENGES
The above description of the transition into priestly ministry and life hints at the multiple tasks and challenges that face the newly ordained. Some tasks are of a directly practical nature. They are important because they have to do with basic functioning as a priest. Other tasks and challenges concerning the appropriation of priestly identity are less visible and less susceptible to empirical verification but are critical and urgent because they are so foundational.

Practical Tasks and Challenges
An initial practical task is to bring closure to the seminary experience. As happy as most are to leave a seminary program to begin direct service as a priest, they may also sense loss in a leave-taking that causes some grieving. If, as part of that process, the newly ordained can summon gratitude by identifying the graces of the years of preparation, that can anchor hope as they begin to navigate through unknown or, at least, unfamiliar waters.

Another practical task is to get to know the new parish community and staff—something of its history, its current make-up, and its graces and struggles.

Newly ordained also need to begin to work, that is, to apply the knowledge and skills that they have acquired in the seminary. A good seminary program will have launched them into the process of linking theory and practice, but now they need to do so more intensively. Translating theory into practice is never a simple matter. The challenge is especially true in priestly ministry. It entails learning from and in the experience of ministry in order to grow in a prudential wisdom that can apply book knowledge in practical and effective ways. Some things can only be learned on-site: the special procedures of a given parish and rectory, collaboration with other staff members, the art of teaching in a classroom and working with youth, care of the sick and grieving parishioners at a time of tragedy, management of conflict, the ability to work with difficult people, and elements of parish administration.

As newly ordained confront these myriad practical tasks and challenges, they are also challenged to learn how to stay centered in what really matters, the heart of their mission as priests. That means, for example, holding fast to a rhythm and pattern of prayer in daily life.

Tasks and Challenges Concerning Identity

In addition to the practical tasks and challenges of beginning priestly ministry in a parish, newly ordained priests face the challenge of growing into a new identity as priests. The process of appropriating a new identity as a priest unfolds both in the interior life of priests as well as in their external and visible ministry and life.

Interior Identity: Because of the consecration that they receive through the conferral of the sacrament of holy orders, priests *are* different. *Pastores Dabo Vobis*, following the seventh proposition of the 1990 Synod, offers the following synthesis:

> It is within the Church's mystery, as a mystery of Trinitarian communion in missionary tension, that every Christian identity is revealed, and likewise the specific identity of the priest and his ministry. Indeed, the priest, by virtue of the consecration which he receives in the Sacrament of Orders, is sent forth by the Father through the mediatorship of Jesus Christ, to whom he is configured in a special way as Head and Shepherd of his people, in order to live and work by the power of the Holy Spirit in service of the Church and for the salvation of the world. (PDV, no. 12 [*Propositio 7*])

Priests, by their ordination, are configured to Jesus Christ, Head and Shepherd, for the sake of mission to the Church and world. This is how they *are* because of ordination. That new way of being, however, does not automatically translate into a new sense of self, a new psychological and spiritual identity. In fact, that internalization and appropriation of what has happened through ordination is a task that lies ahead of those who have been ordained.

In a way that parallels the mystagogical task of the neophytes newly initiated into the mysteries of Christ on Holy Saturday, newly ordained priests are summoned to understand, claim, and deepen what has *already* happened to them in sacred ordination. This is the task of claiming priestly identity interiorly. It

44

means coming to a new, internalized sense of self as *being* in conformity to Christ. Also linked to priestly identity is conformity to Christ in *doing* what he did, so that priests show their "loving concern to the point of a total gift of self for the flock . . ." (PDV, no. 15). This means that in addition to an internalized sense of self as conformed to Christ Head and Shepherd, an internalized and cultivated disposition to give oneself as Christ did also is present. In other words, at an interior level, priests, especially newly ordained, begin to appropriate a new *identity* in Christ and a correlative *commitment* to give of themselves as he did.

Exterior Identity: Newly ordained priests have the task of internalizing their new identity and commitment that flows from ordination. They also have the task of appropriating and living the more external dimensions of their priestly identity that stem from their unique relationships to the bishop and presbyterate and to the Church.

Through ordination priests come into a new identity of belonging to a presbyterate led by its bishop. This relationship stems from their sacramental participation in the presbyteral order. At its deepest level, presbyteral identity in communion with the bishop has sacramental roots. This is clearly stated in *Pastores Dabo Vobis*, no. 17: "By its very nature, the ordained ministry can be carried out only to the extent that the priest is united to Christ through sacramental participation in the priestly order, and thus to the extent that he is in hierarchical communion with his own Bishop. The ordained ministry has a radical *'communitarian form'* and can only be carried out as 'a collective work.'"

In addition to the presbyteral identity forged in sacramental participation, a shared identity accompanies the common work of ministry, an identity that belongs to those who serve collaboratively in the mission of the Church as bishop and priests. They do so out of a shared sense of responsibility for the flock entrusted to them.

Finally, the presbyterate with its bishop can claim a fraternal identity, which means that the sacramental and ministerial bonds are strengthened by the care and solicitude they have for one another (cf. PO, no. 8). It is a task and challenge for newly ordained priests to claim their priestly identity through their sacramental, ministerial, and fraternal connections with the bishop and the presbyterate.

Newly ordained also claim their priestly identity in a more exterior way as they serve the Church at large and their parish in particular. Ordination locates priests in the Church and in relationship to the Church (*in ecclesia . . . erga ecclesiam* [cf. PDV, no. 16 (*Propositio* 7)]) as a sacramental representation of Christ. The ordained priesthood is sacramental because it is conferred by a sacrament and because priests themselves are "sacramental" signs of Christ. Priests' sacramental existence, which precisely as sacramental is exterior and public, gives rise to their identity and is manifested in their service and more general relationship to the Church they serve.

Newly ordained priests grapple with the sacramental and external dimensions of their identity through the new roles and functions that they exercise in a community of faith. These new roles include preachers, presiders, confessors, counselors, teachers, and administrators.

At the same time, newly ordained do not function independently nor in isolation. Generally, they serve with at least one other priest and, most often, with a parish staff. Their task and challenge is to claim and understand their priestly identity in a way that stays true to their sacramental existence and also enables them to serve collaboratively with others, both ordained and non-ordained, for the good of the whole Church. There is a shared task and challenge for the parish, the ministerial staff, and the newly ordained: to listen, to learn, to dialogue, and to stay faithful to the God-given mission and life of the Church.

Celibate Identity: Newly ordained have been prepared for consecrated celibacy in the seminary, have made the public commitment at ordination, and have lived celibately prior to ordination. There is a difference, however, between preparing for celibacy in a seminary context and living out the commitment in the midst of serving the Church as priest. The newly ordained find themselves in the challenging role of being a public person. It is a difficult task to learn how to be a loving and caring priest for significant numbers of people while maintaining appropriate pastoral and interpersonal boundaries. Such challenges are best faced under the supervision of a mentor, pastor, or other delegated supervisor.

The newly ordained have the task and challenge to learn how to love the Church with an undivided and generous heart. *Pastores Dabo Vobis*, no. 29, says, "The Church, as the Spouse of Jesus Christ, wishes to be loved by the priest in the total and exclusive manner in which Jesus Christ her Head and Spouse loved her. Priestly celibacy, then, is the gift of self *in* and *with* Christ *to* his Church and expresses the priest's service to the Church in and with the Lord." The purity, detachment, direction of one's sexuality, and generosity that this love requires are learned by the newly ordained as they serve the people of God. The task and the challenge is, in effect, to learn the integrating path of pastoral charity in its very practice (cf. PDV, no. 23).

SPIRITUAL CONCERNS: TEMPTATIONS, GRACES, DISCERNMENT

The transition into priestly ministry and life is not simply a transition into professional life, that is, the beginning of a new job. It marks a place on the journey in faith of spiritual transformation. As other spiritual moments of importance, this one has its particular temptations, its offers of grace, and its need for discernment.

Temptations

Temptation is a testing, and this seems to be a common experience for newly ordained. The test comes in the form of disillusionment, struggle, or even crisis. It may occur from three to eighteen months after a parochial assignment has begun. Sometimes, it represents a brief moment, other times it is more protracted.

The shape of temptation varies. It may take the form of doubts about one's abilities to meet the kind and quantity of human and spiritual need that is so readily manifest in parish life. It may have to do with rectory living conditions, such as a lack of privacy, a difficult or idiosyncratic pastor, or the "foreignness" of the parish cultural environment. The shape of temptation may be related to the difficulty of finding one's role on a parish staff. It may be connected to a sense of separation and distance from peers and important friends. It can strike at the very heart of priestly ministry and life, as one comes to a deepening awareness of the extraordinary mission given to priests. Grasping the idea that one's mission is not one's own but Christ's can stir up a deep sense of inadequacy and discouragement, if not panic.

Another form of temptation presents itself without any sense of anxiety. Indeed, it is quite the opposite of anxious concern about one's adequacy or ability. It is the temptation to superficial enthusiasm. The first flush of priestly ministry can engender a "high," an ego-stroking sense that one can "take on the world." It is a bent toward self-sufficiency in ministry based on the initial positive responses evoked from people. It leads priests to let go of learning in the course of ministry and to relying altogether too much on their own abilities and ingenuity. In short, it is the temptation to deny grace in the practical order.

Another form of temptation stems from the understandable insecurity of those recently ordained. Faced with so much that is so new, multiple demands, and the often unrealistic expectations of even well-intentioned people, newly ordained priests can be tempted to lock into controllable frameworks, familiar routines, and predictable patterns of ordering reality. A kind of inflexible legalism sometimes is a manifestation of this form of temptation. Not only is it a poor psychological adaptation, it is also a spiritually regressive move that places *my* control of circumstances over *my* surrender to God's will.

A final form of temptation is connected to the multiple and complex set of demands that rush upon newly ordained. Because of the complexity and intensity that they experience in their ministry and lives, they may be tempted to assume a reactive stance toward life and people. Their reactions can be disproportionate to the objective pastoral realities of their situation.

These temptations, as described, highlight possible areas of testing that belong especially to the experience of transition into priestly ministry and life. In the experience of newly ordained and their bishops, more personal forms of temptation may arise now (or later) as they face inclinations in themselves or in other priests toward destructive behavior, such as the violation of sexual boundaries, substance abuse, gambling, and the like. Awareness of such experiences or inclinations may be jarring for the newly ordained and will require particular attention and support.

The experience of temptation is a critical moment in the ongoing formation of newly ordained priests. Just as the temptations of Jesus at the beginning of his public ministry were the occasion to anchor his identity as the obedient Son of the Father who was fully willing to carry out the mission entrusted to him, the experience of temptations for the newly ordained can be an occasion to deepen and consolidate their already-made commitment.

Graces

Grace is, of course, the very life of God, Father, Son, and Holy Spirit dwelling within us. That is the incalculable gift given to us who are reborn in the waters of baptism. There are also graces: particular gifts that point to their source in God and mark the journey of our lives.

The transition into priesthood is an occasion of grace, a time when particular gifts of God are manifest and take hold of the life and heart of priests who journey with their people to God. These particular graces need to be named, received with gratitude, and returned to God through service to his holy people.

The particular graces of priestly ministry and life, even as it begins, are numerous. Here, we identify only three, but they seem especially important: (1) the grace of new beginnings and growth, (2) the grace of vulnerability, and (3) the grace of community.

The transition into priesthood certainly marks a new personal, professional, and spiritual beginning. Accompanying the new beginning is an infusion of new life and prospects of growth. Humanly and personally, the new beginning beckons priests to an expanded and deepened sense of life, the natural correlative of priestly ministry as a deep interpersonal engagement. Professionally, as we have already seen, the beginning of priestly ministry ushers a season of remarkable growth in embracing a role, in participating in activities, in translating theory into action, in developing skills, and in growing in practical wisdom. Spiritually, the new beginning signaled by ordination draws the newly ordained more closely to Christ in whose name and person they serve. The grace of beginnings is really the gift of possibilities for growth.

It is neither easy nor pleasant to feel vulnerable. Still, the time of vulnerability can be a holy season of grace. Newly ordained priests are surely vulnerable in notable ways. Their inexperience, the many new unknowns at the beginning of priestly ministry, and their unproven abilities to cope, respond, and succeed all make them especially vulnerable. The particular grace of their vulnerability rests in a renewed sense of dependence on God. Just as confidence in one's own abilities recedes, a greater openness to the action of God is possible. The grace of vulnerability is, in effect, a gift of greater reliance on him in whom all things are possible.

The grace of community is a deepened re-connection with the body of Christ to which the newly ordained belong and which now, as priests, they serve. In these new relationships to the church community, newly ordained discover the many ways that the gifts of God are at work; their ministry in the community becomes a source of their edification and inspiration.

Discernment

Discernment or the testing of the spirits means sifting through the experiences of ministry and life to determine what is of God and what is not of God. It is not so much, as popular understanding would have it, "figuring things out" as allowing God's truth to surface in a process of humble but alert noticing.

Newly ordained will inevitably feel the tug and pull of various spirits or inclinations leading them in different directions. What is genuine, authentic, and holy? What is not so helpful in the spiritual and ministerial journey? What, in fact, tends toward a dangerous derailment of the journey?

An initial movement is to identify resistances on the journey. For example, *Pastores Dabo Vobis* indicates that the very idea of ongoing formation may be a point of resistance for the newly ordained. They may have "a certain sense of 'having had enough'" (PDV, no. 76) in their seminary experience. Other points of resistance might include a false sense of independence, a fear of uncovering inadequacies, and an unwillingness to rely on a larger wisdom.

The process of discernment or maintaining a discerning heart assumes that one is engaged in and faithful to a life of prayer. If, at the beginning of one's priestly ministry, the sudden surge of pastoral demands obliterates the regularity of personal prayer or if the positive response of people to one's initial efforts seems to diminish prayer's necessity, then discernment cannot happen.

Discernment for the newly ordained and for everyone occurs in an ecclesial context in which we rely on the Holy Spirit at work in the community of faith and among particular believers in the community. So, discernment will also assume a willingness to share with others and to rely on them. It is not simply a solitary process. It needs spiritual direction, holy friendship, and the fraternity of other priests. Discernment requires a humble willingness to be self disclosing; it is not simply about psychological facts or states but about the movements of grace and the inclinations to sin.

Programmatic Responses to Transition into Priesthood: The event of transition into priesthood, its tasks and challenges, and its spiritual dimensions are numerous and complex. Each diocese can respond to its newly ordained in some organized program that respects the particularity of the diocese and the specific character of the newly ordained. Programs—seminars, retreats, workshops, study days, "mentoring"—will vary. A constant element holds: those *persons* involved in the programs are those individuals and groups who contribute decisively to the ongoing formation of the newly ordained. The focus of this section is mainly on the persons involved in ongoing formation and less on the design of specific programs that can and do vary according to local circumstance.

Among those involved in ongoing formation are the newly ordained priests themselves, both as individuals and as a group; the bishop; the presbyterate generally and some priests specifically; and the parish staff and the parish at large.

Individual Newly Ordained Priests

Pastores Dabo Vobis, no. 79, locates primary responsibility for ongoing formation in priests themselves: "The priest himself, *the individual priest . . . is the person primarily responsible in the Church for ongoing formation.* Truly each priest has the duty, rooted in the Sacrament of Holy Orders, to be faithful to the gift God has given him and to respond to the call for daily conversion which comes with the gift itself."

The responsibility and the agency of individual priests is manifested above all in their deliberate commitment to grow personally, intellectually, pastorally, and spiritually. That commitment is real and operative on a personal level, if priests are, in fact, praying daily, cultivating a reflective approach to ministry by retrieving important experiences and scrutinizing them, and by the practice of personal study of theological, pastoral, and spiritual issues.

When newly ordained priests take hold of their own ongoing formation, good things happen. Their special gifts to the Church emerge. They offer a fresh perspective, an encouragement extended to young men to consider a vocation to priestly ministry, and a general renewal of energy and enthusiasm in the local church community.

Peers

The newly ordained form a distinct cohort. Often in a given diocese, they share a common formational history and common experiences in entering priestly ministry. The gathering of the newly ordained can have powerful formational significance.

The newly ordained can share their experiences and so break out of the isolation that can be a hazard of beginning priestly ministry. The sharing of experiences in a proper spiritual and theological context can also tap a Spirit-prompted wisdom that leads to deeper understanding and an enriched return to priestly ministry.

When the newly ordained come together to pray over their experiences of priestly ministry, they make themselves more available to grace at work in their lives and more open to the conversion of heart to which their service calls them. In addition, the gathering of the newly ordained provides a mutual support that is spiritual, moral, and authentically human. Such support is the necessary and encouraging context of ongoing formation.

The Bishop and the Presbyterate

The bishop plays a decisive role in the ongoing formation of the newly ordained. He does so both directly and indirectly. When he meets with the newly ordained individually and in groups, he is a directly encouraging and challenging presence in their formational journey. When he reminds the presbyterate to welcome their new brothers and to help them in their continuing initiation into priestly ministry and life, he creates a climate that enables ongoing formation to take place.

From among the presbyterate, one priest will play an essential role in the ongoing formation of the newly ordained, and he will do so on a daily basis. That is the first pastor. His formational impact is inestimable. Ideally, he will be chosen because he is known to possess qualities helpful in initiating newly ordained into priestly ministry. The first pastor welcomes the newly ordained into the parish community, guides them in the functions of priestly service, provides a connection to the larger presbyterate, and models both immediately and intensely how priesthood can be lived.

Experience also indicates that a priest-mentor can be very helpful in the ongoing formation of newly ordained priests. He is neither the first pastor nor a spiritual director but a priest of "exemplary life and pastoral zeal" (DMLP, no. 82), who, precisely because he is not on-site, can help the newly ordained sort out their experiences and see them with greater objectivity. The priest-mentor brings a wisdom born of experience as well as a sense of the life of the local church. He engages the newly ordained in conversation about his ministry, his sense of priestly identity, rectory life, and other important issues. The priest-mentor is available to answer questions from the newly ordained or to help them process unfamiliar and perhaps difficult situations.

A spiritual director, ordinarily a priest, contributes significantly to the ongoing formation of newly ordained priests. The spiritual director provides a focus and a reminder of the primacy of the spiritual life: the necessity of the Morning and Evening Prayer of the Church, especially the Liturgy of the Hours; the value of particular practices such as retreats, days of renewal, and devotions; the integration of all ministry and life in the Lord's paschal mystery; the centrality of the word of God found in the Sacred Scriptures; and the invitation to an ever-fuller and deeper participation in the sacramental life of the Church, especially in the Eucharist and the sacrament of reconciliation.

Another priest of importance for the newly ordained is the priest responsible for the ongoing formation of priests. He arranges for particular programs of study and prayer for the newly ordained but also integrates them into the offerings that are made to the presbyterate at large. The diocesan priest-director listens to their needs and tries to tailor programs accordingly. He also presents the needs of the diocese to them and challenges them to prepare themselves to meet those needs through prayer and study.

Parish Staff and the Parish at Large

In addition to the pastor, newly ordained priests very often arrive in a parish with a developed staff. Some may be ordained priests or deacons, and others are not ordained but specially trained, for example, in religious education, liturgy, or social outreach. Through a process of honest dialogue and sincere collaboration with the staff, the newly ordained priest can find himself more readily able to claim his own unique priestly identity and to affirm and encourage other service in the Church.

Parishioners, who generally take great pride in having a newly ordained among them, can also provide immense formational support through their words and prayers. They can also provide considerable practical assistance through the feedback they give to newly ordained, for example, concerning clarity of communication, availability, sensitivity to needs, and skills in organization. If this feedback is organized and systematic, it can be especially useful to one who is beginning priestly ministry.

Programs for the ongoing formation of newly ordained priests are necessary. Their format and shape, however, vary according to local need and resources, the number of newly ordained, and whether they are older (typically aged 35-50) and in a second career. More foundational and constant amid the variations are the people who interact with the newly ordained in programs and in the course of their priestly ministry and life.

ACCOUNTABILITY

Accountability, as noted in part one, is a very important word in the consideration of the ongoing formation of priests at every age and specifically for newly ordained priests. Without accountability eloquent words about ongoing formation and elaborate programs amount to nothing. With accountability there is a real possibility for growth and change, indeed, for a conversion of heart.

Pope John Paul II indicates in *Pastores Dabo Vobis*, no. 79, that unless the values of ongoing formation are internalized, external ecclesiastical norms and expectations will not have much effect. A kind of accountability needs to be established by a bishop and his presbyterate and shaped by the Church at large, which has a great stake in the ongoing formation of her priests. This accountability has to do with norms and expectations, which give voice to values that the Church holds for and in her priests. If it is to be effective, the norms and expectations of accountability need to be clear. Even more important, they need a spiritual foundation, the kind that St. Paul seems to supply when he frequently gives an account of his ministry.

CONCLUSION

Newly ordained experience a single transition from the major seminary to their first parochial assignment. That single transition, however, contains many aspects and multiple implications for ongoing formation. It is important not to lose the central point in considering this complexity. A constant thread woven through the various dimensions of experience is that of integration, linking "who I am" and "what I do for the sake of the mission," drawing together in integrity priestly identity and service to the mission of Jesus Christ.

In effect, all our considerations return to a center, the meaning of ongoing formation as Pope John Paul II describes it in *Pastores Dabo Vobis*, no. 73: "Ongoing formation has as its aim that *the priest become a believer and ever more of one:* that he grow in understanding of who he truly is, seeing things with the eyes of Christ."

B. Priests in Transition: Ongoing Formation and Changes of Assignment

INTRODUCTION

One of the most poignant discourses in the Acts of the Apostles is Paul's farewell speech at Miletus (20:17-35), where he takes leave of the presbyters of Ephesus. Indeed, he says that he *must* go: "Now, compelled by the Spirit, I am going to Jerusalem" (20:22). His future is uncertain, even tenuous: "What will happen to me there I do not know, except that in one city after another the holy Spirit has been warning me that imprisonment and hardships await me" (20:22-23). His faith and sense of mission carry him through the transition: "Yet I consider life of no importance to me, if only I may finish my course and the ministry that I received from the Lord Jesus, to bear witness to the gospel of God's grace" (20:24).

Paul's experience resonates with that of priests changing assignments. Often, some necessity marks their change, perhaps because of a diocesan policy of limited terms in assignments. Priests frequently experience uncertainty about "the next move." Finally, like Paul's departure, priests' experience of an assignment change contains significant spiritual and religious possibilities. The time of change offers formational opportunities, an occasion when priests can open themselves to God's transforming action within them.

The next section will describe the event of changing assignments, followed by a second section on the tasks and challenges that accompany change. A third section will explore the spiritual dimensions of this experience under the themes of temptation, grace, and discernment. A final section will identify possible programs and responses to the formational needs of priests in transition.

EVENT

Other parts of this basic plan for ongoing formation are tied to specific chronological points in the life and faith journey of priests. Transitions in priesthood, however, occur in every stage of life. Age and experience may shape the way one meets the prospect and challenge of change, but basic dynamics remain the same.

Any description of the event of transition in the life of diocesan priests must also take into account the various forms that such a transition can take: parochial vicar to pastor (more on this later); parochial vicar in one place to parochial vicar in another; pastor in one place to pastor in another; parochial ministry to non-parochial ministry, for example, in education, health care, or administration; non-parochial ministry to a return to parochial ministry; service in the diocese to priestly service outside the diocese, for example, in the military, the missions, or on loan to another diocese; and a return to the diocese after service outside the diocese. The parochial vicar and pastor changes are the most common, but the others fill out the picture of changing assignments.

In describing the event of transition, it is important to note the two dimensions that changing assignments entails. In one sense, the move from one assignment to another belongs to the personnel or placement system. Changing assignments results from an administrative decision based on needs in parishes and institutions, the diocesan mission, and the available personnel resources. Viewed in this perspective, assignment changes parallel processes in business, education, government, or the military. In the case of priests, however, there is an added dimension.

In addition to the administrative dimension, priests' assignment changes include a formational dimension as well, a spiritual moment that marks their faith journeys. The change signals an opportunity to revisit and deepen the integration of priestly identity and service, of who I am and what I do for the sake of the mission.

In other words, the event of transition for priests is or, at least, can be a holy moment. This prospect echoes the many biblical stories of movement and relocation, for example, the story of Abraham's journey to a new land, Israel's liberating journey of Exodus from Egypt to the Promised Land, the journey of Jesus to Jerusalem, and the missionary journeys of Paul. All of these journeys are formative and transformative.

The biblical journeys of faith and the experience of priests' transitions share common moments: departing, moving, beginning. There is closure that includes leave-taking and the actual departure. Moving or being in movement both from and towards is proper to the transition. Finally, after the arrival, the re-initiation to ministry and life can begin.

The accounts of the biblical journeys as well as the accounts of priests' experience indicate that change is emotionally costly and often painful. At the same time, it can yield immense gains and effect an infusion of new life. It is a time of opportunity.

TASKS AND CHALLENGES
The tasks and challenges of transition can be clustered around the basic moments of transition: departing, moving, beginning. Each moment combines tasks and challenges that are both psychological and spiritual. The psychological task is to accept and manage change. The spiritual task is to respond to God's invitation *in* the change process.

Leaving With Deliberateness

A deliberate leave-taking is a first task for priests in transition. It is a sign of human sensitivity not to rush off. The farewell discourse of Jesus in John's Gospel (Jn 14-17) tells us that a deliberate leave-taking can be a holy event.

Deliberate leave-taking includes several steps. First, it means taking time to say goodbye, to face people directly, and to say the word that marks change in one's relationship with them. Often, they need to hear an assurance that there will still be a connection, not as it was but in some altered form. Friends and trusted colleagues, for example, need reassurance that they are not going to be left behind, although adjustments to relationships need to be made. Because the human inclination is often to avoid painful goodbyes, it is a task and a challenge to face change so directly.

Another, often challenging task of leave-taking is to let go of past hurts or to try to heal them. Hurts have to do with unfinished business, and unless they are discarded or resolved, they can continue to have a negative impact even in a new situation. Hurts also come when the leave-taking is not voluntary, but requested under obedience. Every departure contains its own call to reconciliation.

Although gratitude may rise within oneself spontaneously, vocalizing gratitude or saying thank you is a deliberate task and challenge. Through expressed, deliberate gratitude, priests affirm their experience of priestly ministry, acknowledge people who have been at the heart of their ministry, and celebrate the workings of God's grace. Conversely, it is important to allow people to say thank you to their priest, so that he can know what he has meant to them and they can acknowledge what God has done through him.

Finally, a great task of leaving with deliberateness embraces everything else—the goodbyes, the connections, the reconciliation, the thanks—in some ritualized form. This usually includes a Mass and a party. These are not simply *pro forma* events. For Catholics who prize sacramentality, community, and tradition, the ritualization of departure is an essential ingredient that makes leave-taking whole and complete.

Moving Graciously

Tasks and challenges belong not only to leave-taking but also to the very process of moving. The great challenge in moving is to do so with grace. That means with God's grace and with a personal sense of gracefulness. Moving graciously begins with a sense of peace and avoids, at all costs, a hurried, frantic pace. Our own nervousness can accelerate the pace and cause us to miss the opportunities latent in the experience of change.

Only in peace and calm can priests retrieve the personal, pastoral, and spiritual opportunities that change affords. For example, the very process of moving can occasion a review or gathering of ministry and commitment. In a calm environment, change can draw us into a deep sense of recollection—literally, inner gathering. It can also invite us to re-affirm our commitments and re-dedicate ourselves in priestly ministry, while also calling us to realign the way we do things or to a fuller conversion of heart.

The moving process is a particular challenge to diocesan priests whose incardination in a diocese defines them in terms of local geography and inclines them to a certain stability. The move from one assignment to another sharpens the challenge to cultivate a missionary sense and a wider outreach.

Beginning Anew

Obvious tasks and challenges present themselves at the beginning of a new assignment. Simply getting to know people, familiarizing oneself with local history, and sensing the culture of the new place and people are practical, necessary, and rather obvious tasks and challenges. Yet there are tasks and challenges of beginning anew that are more subtle.

An internal challenge of beginning anew is to use one's past experience—to profit from it and to employ it effectively but, at the same time, not to be bound by it. In other words, the ideal is to use one's experience but not to try to repeat it, to draw on the past but with great openness to a new future. In the traditional spiritual language of gifts and virtues, this is the cultivation of wisdom and prudence, a large perspective born of experience and a practical habit of doing things the right way (*recta ratio agibilium*), again cultivated through practical experience.

Another internal task and challenge is that of personal reinvestment in a new situation. The task is to give oneself over to a new people, a new set of circumstances, and a new call of God in the situation.

SPIRITUAL CONCERNS: TEMPTATIONS, GRACES, DISCERNMENT

The Bible alerts us to the many spiritual possibilities latent in journeys and changes. We have already noted some examples that stretch from Abraham's move to a new land to Paul's missionary journeys. When spiritual concerns are intimately attached to our experience, we can be sure that elements of temptation, the assurance of grace, and the invitation to discernment will inevitably be present. And so they are.

Temptations

The change process alters life and ministry patterns, predictable routines, and ordinary expectations. Everything is shaken up. This is a ripe time for temptation, the testing that invites us to re-affirm our basic commitments that transcend particular circumstances.

Change of assignment marks a loss, and this in turn can cause a loss of heart, an inclination to discouragement. The temptation to discouragement can be linked to leaving behind one's accomplishments with the prospect of having to start all over again. Or, alternately, at the end of an assignment, one realizes how much more there is to do, and there is an abiding sense of unfinished business. In either case, temptation arrives as a pull to discouragement, to lose heart.

Another form of temptation has to do with the inclination to hold on to previous securities. It may take the form, for example, of a clinging attachment to the previous parish experience, so much so that it can impair or even stymie a full move into a new assignment.

One can also be tempted not to face reality. Avoiding the issues of change often manifests itself as an unwillingness to adapt to a new situation or to negotiate new realities. That inclination to inflexibility is really an unwillingness to stay with what is, to want to create one's own world.

The loss that accompanies change can tempt one to an unproductive form of anger. Sometimes this is compounded by a sense of injustice in the placement process. If one feels treated unfairly in the process, past hurts can emerge at the time of transition to fuel a spirit of resentment.

Finally, a very human and understandable temptation is to fear. The process of change uncovers our fragility and vulnerability. These naturally draw us toward fear, the fear that Jesus frequently seeks to dispel in his disciples and apostles. Regularly in the Gospels, we hear him say to disciples, "Do not be afraid." The very following of and being sent out in mission from Jesus uncovers our naked humanity and can draw us into terrible fear. It is a longstanding temptation.

Grace
The change of assignment process is not simply an occasion of temptation. It is also and more deeply an occasion of grace, when God's presence is more manifest and when we recognize that we move not simply by our own power but in virtue of the one who loves us.

The primary grace of changing assignments is participation in the paschal mystery of the Lord. The change that implies loss includes a kind of dying. It also affords a promise and an invitation to new life. In a way that is both remarkable and quite specific, the paschal mystery takes palpable hold of priests so disposed in the change process. Paul expresses this eloquently in 2 Corinthians, chapter 4, and it became the *leitmotif* of the document *The Spiritual Renewal of the American Priesthood* (1973), which was sponsored by the U.S. bishops' conference.

Another tangible grace in the change process is the opportunity to renew one's commitment. This new chance to take up one's ministry and life with deliberateness comes as a great gift. Just as shifting circumstances in a marriage—a first child, a new job, a death in the family, the empty nest, the aging process—occasion a renewal of the commitment of a couple, so too, priests' shifts of circumstance that are occasioned by a different assignment become an occasion of grace for renewing commitment.

One final grace needs to be named here, although frequently there are others present in the change process. As priests leave an assignment and take up a new one, they extend the reach of their mission. Diocesan priests do not often consider themselves to be missionaries, but they do participate, as indeed the entire Church participates, in the universal mission. To move to a new place and to begin anew awakens the missionary dimension of priests' vocations, ministry, and lives. This is a true grace or gift, a participation in the very mission of Jesus Christ: "As the Father has sent me, so I send you" (Jn 20:21).

Discernment

Psychology offers human help to individuals who struggle to adapt and adjust, especially to new and difficult circumstances in life. It offers a hope for living life more efficiently, with less drag due to the psychopathology of daily life that can weigh us down. Priests in transition may avail themselves of the help afforded by psychology, which can be for the good. This help, however, is insufficient; another dimension of faith is not touched with psychological methods. In faith, we believe that our lives are more than the sum of biological, psychological, and sociological processes. They are a journey to God. Discernment, the testing of the spirits, enables us to identify and embrace our lives of journey to God by viewing events and movements in faith.

A first task of discernment, which can happen in personal prayer or in the dialogue of spiritual direction, is to uncover or discover the meaning of the change or transition in assignment for one's relationship with God. Our destiny is union with the Triune God—Father, Son, and Holy Spirit. Even now we are in relationship with God, although the shape and dimensions of that relationship are not always immediately evident. Discernment reads events with the eyes of faith and deciphers how an event such as transition bears on our relationship with God, how it might draw us closer to God, and what response it summons from us. This is the foundational task of discernment for priests in transition.

Another discernment process reads the situation of change in faith and identifies the kind of apostolic detachment to which we might be called. Every movement forward in the spiritual journey is also a departure, a letting go. This does not happen in generalities but in the particularities of our ministry and lives. So it is essential to identify, that is, to discern the precise call to detachment that belongs to us in the change process. Some detachment may clearly and easily be identified because it involves external realities. A more subtle and significant invitation to inner detachment also exists, for example, from reluctance, fear, or old securities. This detachment is apostolic because it connects closely with the mission.

The discernment process may touch on very practical matters. For example, although one is called to detachment and departure, some continuity and connection can and ought to remain, but to what extent? In what way? For how long? Human wisdom offers a perspective on these questions. God's holy wisdom offers another perspective that enables us to identify God's will and direction. That is how discernment works.

If our ministry and lives are not simply constituted by a string of events, if indeed they are constituted by a sustained journey into God, then we need to notice in faith what is happening. Thus, every movement, including priests' changes of assignment, becomes an occasion for living out an ongoing conversion of life.

PROGRAMMATIC RESPONSES TO TRANSITIONS IN PRIESTLY MINISTRY
Specific programs for priests in transition obviously do not create themselves. Someone needs to develop and manage programs that can be helpful in addressing the event, the tasks and challenges, and the discernment that are part of the transition process. Programs will, however, flow more easily if the essential and formational ingredients for assisting priests are present. There are four such essential ingredients that can direct local programming, which must respect particular needs and available resources. The ingredients are (1) sharing of experience, (2) apt solitude, (3) appropriate breaks, and (4) follow-up.

These ingredients and the programs that flow from them should always be in service to the recurring theme of priestly ongoing formation: the integration of who I am and what I do for the sake of the mission. That purpose is necessary to align programs properly and to prevent their running away on their own.

Sharing of Experience
In large measure, managing the transition process belongs to the individual. It should not, however, lead priests into isolation. On the contrary, the sharing of experience helps priests to contextualize their own particular journeys and to

draw strength and support from others. The sharing of experience may include dialogue with other peers who are experiencing or who have recently experienced a change in assignment. Peer sharing can be both comforting and challenging. Sharing experience may also happen in the context of conversation with a priest-mentor or a spiritual director or friends, whether lay or priest, who care about the priest in transition.

Apt Solitude

Although solitude cannot be programmed, the conditions for it can be arranged. It is an essential formational ingredient in the change process. In solitude and quiet, priests can notice what is happening in their ministry and lives. In solitude they can move beyond managing the transition to allow themselves to be carried by the love of God and the faith of the people they serve. In solitude they can come to terms with the stable center of their lives in Jesus Christ who is beyond all change.

Appropriate Breaks

Related to solitude is the need in the change process for breaks, intervals that allow for the formational impact of transition to happen. In some instances, sabbaticals are an appropriate break in the transition process, an extended period of study, prayer, and rest between assignments. Sometimes, a retreat creates space in the transition. An extended vacation can also be useful. Whatever the form, and that will vary according to individual circumstance, appropriate breaks are essential to engage the formational process that is latent in transitions.

Follow-Up

Placement systems generally focus on "getting someone to some place." Follow-up may or may not happen, but to tap the formational possibilities of transition, it is essential. A designated person, for example, the bishop, a clergy vicar, a placement board member, or someone in the system, needs to accompany the person in transition. The designated person can offer encouragement and provide some challenge to the person in transition. He may also help to identify and facilitate the need for time away on vacation or on retreat. Most importantly, the designated person can remind the person in transition that what is happening is a holy moment, a part of the Church's larger mission and an offer of grace. As noted earlier, accountability to Christ, the Church, the bishop, and the people served must mark the process of growing in and through the transitional process.

C. Priests as Pastors: Ongoing Formation and the First Pastorate

INTRODUCTION

In his farewell speech to the presbyters of Ephesus, Paul exhorts them with striking words that still speak clearly and forcefully to pastors in today's Church: "Keep watch over yourselves and over the whole flock of which the holy Spirit has appointed you overseers, in which you tend the church of God that he acquired with his own blood" (Acts 20:28).

All priests in virtue of their ordination act in the name and person of Jesus Christ, Head and Shepherd of the Church. All priests are to proclaim the word, to celebrate the sacraments, and to share in the pastoral care and governance of God's holy people. Pastors of parishes, however, do so under a particular title and with a specific set of responsibilities. Canon 519 explains who a pastor is and what he does: "The pastor is the proper shepherd of the parish entrusted to him, exercising pastoral care in the community entrusted to him under the authority of the diocesan bishop in whose ministry of Christ he has been called to share; in accord with the norm of law he carries out for his community the duties of teaching, sanctifying and governing, with the cooperation of other presbyters or deacons and the assistance of lay members of the Christian faithful."

Diocesan priests generally become pastors after serving as parochial vicars or as associate pastors. The time of service as a parochial vicar, which may vary according to diocesan circumstances from a few years to a dozen or more years, can be seen as a period of being a "pastor in training." It would be most helpful if before becoming a pastor, a priest would have had several assignments, and a few years of experience in the pastoral ministry.

When a parochial vicar is named a pastor, the appointment and move mark an important transition in the priest's life. The office of pastor brings the priest into a new set of responsibilities and a new focus for his priestly identity and service. Appointment to the pastorate rekindles the question of integrating identity and function for the sake of mission—who I am and what I do for the sake of the mission entrusted to the Church. Appointment to the pastorate summons a priest to new growth and development in his humanity, his discipleship, and his priesthood.

The time of entering the first pastorate is a ripe moment for ongoing formation in all its dimensions. Significantly, it can also set a pace for how growth, development, and formation will happen in the years ahead. This is clearly a decisive moment, and it requires care and consideration. Moreover, when a priest moves to his pastorate, he must face the issues already considered in the previous section on transitions in general, in addition to the specific adjustments entailed with pastoring for the first time. This is sometimes overlooked by the priest himself and the people of his new parish.

The following sections follow the pattern of other parts of the *Basic Plan* by describing the event, identifying the tasks and challenges, noting spiritual concerns, and, finally, indicating some program responses.

EVENT

To be named a pastor means assuming a new role or position as well as a new set of responsibilities. These are neither entirely new nor completely unfamiliar to priests who have served and participated in parish life as associates. There is, nevertheless, a real newness in receiving and claiming these as a pastor.

Canon law identifies the new responsibilities as specifications of priestly service *for a particular community*, that is, a parish. Canon 528, for example, identifies the pastor's ministry of the word, which he exercises through preaching, teaching, and evangelizing. That same canon addresses his ministry of sanctification, primarily through the celebration of the sacraments. The following canon (529) describes relational demands of the pastoral office, knowing and being known by the people entrusted to one's care, especially the most vulnerable. Canon 530 describes some specific liturgical functions that belong to the pastor's responsibility. Finally, canon 532 describes the administrative function of the pastor, a set of stewardship responsibilities that seem, in the experience of some, to eclipse all the others: "The pastor represents the parish in all juridic affairs in accord with the norm of law; he is to see to it that the goods of the parish are administered in accord with the norms of cann. 1281-1288."

Clearly, to be named a pastor sets a priest in a new configuration of responsibilities and relationships within a community of people—a parish. The priest is pastor, not in a global or generic sense but very particularly *of this parish*. His ministry and life are intimately tied to the parish. So, in describing the event of becoming a pastor, it may be helpful to identify some key elements of parish life for which the pastor is responsible.

The 1983 *Code of Canon Law* follows the footsteps of Vatican II and describes a parish this way: "A parish is a definite community of the Christian faithful established on a stable basis within a particular church; the pastoral care of the parish is entrusted to a pastor as its own shepherd under the authority of the diocesan bishop" (can. 515, §1). This description highlights the parish as a community of persons, but it also includes structural and institutional dimensions. In the lived experience of Catholic Christian people, the parish is also the place where the Christian message comes alive, the mysteries of Christ are celebrated, and a sense of mission is reinvigorated. In short, the parish is experienced as the place and community that keeps the dynamism of Christianity alive.

The parish, in other words, is a *system*, a *community*, and a *movement*. It is a system because it is a structured institution that provides services and gives the community visibility and a focal point. It is a community because it is constituted by a communion of believers in relationship to each other in faith, sacraments, and mission. It is a movement because it keeps alive aspirations for and alertness to the coming of the reign of God.

To be a pastor of a parish, then, is no simple matter. It means taking responsibility for a reality that is at once a system, a community, and a movement. As a priest, the pastor directs, guides, manages, and governs the parish as a system. As one who acts in the name of and in the person of Jesus Christ, Head and Pastor of the Church, the pastor is a sacramental presence who effectively heads this portion of the Church, this community. As servant of Christ and the Gospel, the pastor works for and serves the parish, keeping it alive to its mission to be salt and leaven in the world, a true movement.

TASKS AND CHALLENGES

Pastors serve the complex realities of parishes. The tasks and challenges they face are shared with all priests but with an added focus on the context of the parish and the assumption of a new sense of responsibility. For example, pastors like all priests have the task and challenge to proclaim the word well in preaching, teaching, catechesis, and spiritual guidance. They do so, however, in the context of knowing *this* community and adapting their method of proclamation to fit its needs.

Pastors exercise a ministry of sanctification by celebrating the sacraments and leading their people in prayer. The universal work of our redemption in Jesus Christ, now extended in time through the power of the Holy Spirit, comes alive in this place, in this parish. Pastors not only celebrate the sacraments but also are the sacramental presence of Jesus Christ, Head and Shepherd, within their community. They guide, direct, and shepherd the parish community as its servant and leader. Specifically, they offer leadership and direction to the structures of parish life, such as, personnel, consultative bodies, different kinds of ministries, volunteers, and also the material goods of the parish.

Clearly, the *pastor loci*—the "pastor of the place"— engages in the priestly tasks of proclamation, sanctification, and governance for this portion of God's people. He does so, however, in communion with the bishop of the diocese, who in turn stands in communion with the universal Church. So, the pastor serves both God's people and the bishop in a focused way in the parish and in an expansive and unitive mode that links the parish with the diocese and the Church universal.

In carrying out these tasks, pastors need skills, for example, in communications and administration. They need practical wisdom, for example, to translate general norms into their particular situation. They need presence and availability to their people, so that they can be effective sacramental signs of the Church's unity and the Good Shepherd's care. Finally, they need spiritual transparency or an evident spirituality that enables them to be unambiguous witnesses of the holy mysteries that they proclaim and celebrate.

In the complexity that is parish life and the multiple tasks of parish priests, the greatest challenge for pastors, especially new ones, is to pay attention to all the dimensions and to do so with a sense of proportion. In this way, no single dimension, such as the pressing needs of administration, captures all the attention or captures it disproportionately. The task then of ongoing formation is to *learn how* to do this and *to be sufficiently spiritually centered*, so that in fact one does it.

SPIRITUAL CONCERNS: TEMPTATIONS, GRACES, DISCERNMENT

The spiritual concerns of pastors, including new pastors, are the same as those of other priests with the added emphasis on the parish community and the sense of responsibility that accompanies the office of pastor. One's ministry and spirituality, always intimately related, are even more closely connected in the life of a pastor who must strive to integrate who he is and what he does for the sake of the mission.

In a pastor's spiritual journey, even from the start, there are temptations, graces, and a call to discernment.

Temptations

Given the immediacy and concreteness of administrative functions, it is tempting to surrender attention and energy to the system side of parish life. A single conflict among staff can be very absorbing. Not having enough money to keep "the operation" going can easily capture full attention. The maintenance, especially of old buildings, can be consuming. A new pastor with little experience in these areas can quickly be drawn into full-time administration.

A related though somewhat different temptation is to be overwhelmed by the complexity of parish life and the tasks that belong to the pastor. Surrendering to this overwhelming complexity can lead a pastor either to immobility or reactivity to whatever crosses his path. In either case, he does not respond freely and thoughtfully out of a deliberate commitment.

A final temptation that can strike a new or experienced pastor is lack of focus. Because of the multiple demands, one can easily forget the point, the purpose, and, really, the sense of the parish's and pastor's mission.

Every temptation is an invitation to a commitment re-affirmed. These temptations of pastoral ministry are no different. They invite pastors to reclaim a singular vision that would guide them through the complexities and vicissitudes of ministry as a pastor. This is Paul's vision that he expresses throughout his writings, for example, in 2 Corinthians 6:3-8: "We cause no one to stumble in anything, in order that no fault may be found with our ministry; on the contrary, in everything we commend ourselves as ministers of God, through much endurance, in afflictions, hardships, constraints, beatings, imprisonments, riots, labors, vigils, fasts; by purity, knowledge, patience, kindness, in a holy spirit, in unfeigned love, in truthful speech, in the power of God; with weapons of righteousness at the right and at the left; through glory and dishonor, insult and praise."

Graces

The particular graces that belong to pastors are common to priests in pastoral ministry but with the added dimension of focus in the parish community. From the beginning, for example, pastors are aware of a great gift: they see, hear, and touch the narrative of God's grace alive in the individuals and community entrusted to their care.

Pastors also experience the blessing of being a person (not the only person, though surely a crucial one) of great significance for the community as a particular instrument of grace. Some of this results from what they do, but much happens simply because of who they are as sacraments of the presence of Jesus Christ, Head and Shepherd. Whatever the shape of the particular grace of being pastor, it draws those who serve into gratitude, a deeper sense of their dependence on God, and a heightened sense of their responsibility before the community of faith.

Discernment

Discernment is the discovery of the direction that God offers us. New and experienced pastors need to engage in the discernment process whether in the context of personal prayer, spiritual direction, conversation with friends, or the prayerful gathering of parishioners, such as the parish pastoral council.

Parish life and the ministry of pastor offer numerous possibilities for personal, professional, and spiritual investment. Surely, a pastor cannot respond to every possibility. The discernment of investment asks the question: Where is God drawing me in this community and through my ministry to give my talents and share my life?

Pastors also bring another kind of question to discernment. By the grace of office and the promise of God to be faithful to those who serve, the pastor can be assured that the Spirit speaks through him in giving a direction to the community. He is, of course, not the only outlet for the Spirit's promptings, but he is an important one. So it is essential that he be alert to the internal movements of the Holy Spirit that may be offering direction for the life of the parish. Discernment detects what those movements are and tests their genuineness.

Because of their position in the community, pastors ought to have a sense of the whole. They can sense the truth of Paul's statement, "To each individual the manifestation of the Spirit is given for some benefit" (1 Cor 12:7). Discernment means deciphering how the gifts of the Spirit are at work in individuals and through individuals in the Church at large. Once discerned, the gifts of the Spirit at work in the parish can be affirmed, celebrated, and encouraged.

Finally, pastors exercise a particular form of discernment in the guidance and governance of a parish community. The New Testament witness, the experience of pastors, and the teachings of the Church, especially in the Second Vatican Council, all converge in affirming that responsibilities for the mission are shared among many in the Church. A fundamental task of discernment for the pastor in communion with others is to determine exactly how those responsibilities are to be shared.

PROGRAMMATIC RESPONSES TO THE FIRST PASTORATE
Programmatic responses reflect the concerns not only of new pastors but of older and more experienced pastors as well. Ongoing formation in a particular aspect may be more critical at a given point, but it remains an abiding concern and need at every moment.

Three general areas of programmatic response to the needs of pastors suggest themselves: (1) skills and knowledge, (2) personal and spiritual growth, and (3) connection with persons of experience.

Skills and Knowledge

A pressing need for a new pastor is to acquire the "know how" of being and functioning as a pastor. Often, this is tied to very specific issues, for example, the business function of pastoring. Pastors need to learn, in some context, basics of financial management, fundamental personnel management, conflict resolution, the organization of meetings, community organization and communication, and the management of volunteers. Pastors need to familiarize themselves with canonical requirements, diocesan regulations, and any civil legal provisions that have a bearing on parish life, such as employment law. Finally, new pastors need to discover ways of knowing and understanding the community in which they serve: demographics, culture, economics, and political realities.

The acquisition of this knowledge and these skills in a short time appears to be an intimidating prospect. Workshops, visits with diocesan and local officials, on-line study, and consultation with experienced pastors can greatly facilitate learning the business function of pastoring.

Still in the realm of knowledge, a new pastor does well to review his study of the Church. Revisiting the Church's convictions about herself as found, for example, in the documents of the Second Vatican Council can provide context and a gentle reminder of what really matters for the mission.

Personal and Spiritual Growth

As a priest begins to pastor a community, he is summoned to new growth and development. Of course, some growth occurs in knowledge and skills as we noted above. Also a deeper invitation to growth exists both personally and spiritually. To be a pastor stretches a priest's humanity as he strives to relate to and care for a community as their father, brother, spouse, and servant. It also becomes an invitation to spiritual growth: greater reliance on God, fuller transparency of the mystery of Christ at work in one's life, a deeper sense of pastoral courage, a more dedicated commitment to intercession on behalf of the community, a strengthened pattern of celibate loving, and more generous self-giving in service.

Human and spiritual growth is not forced or made to happen. The circumstances of life infused with God's grace and our own openness to receive transformation enable it. Some useful means facilitate our receptivity: devoted participation in the sacramental and liturgical life of the Church, a habit of personal prayer, spiritual conversation with friends and confidants, dialogue of spiritual direction, and times of recollection, reflection, and retreat.

Connection With Persons of Experience

In some sense, pastors stand alone as shepherds of the parish communities entrusted to them. This solitary portrait, however, needs significant qualification in light of *Pastores Dabo Vobis*'s important assertion: "The ordained ministry has a radical '*communitarian form*' and can only be carried out as 'a collective work'" (no. 17).

A final programmatic dimension of coming into the first pastorate (and lasting throughout one's time as pastor) is the establishment of connections in the presbyterate. Obviously the bishop under whose authority the pastor serves is a significant person, and ties of connection with him need to be nourished. Other pastors of the diocese can offer wisdom, support, and challenge, and in small groups or as a collective body, pastors should gather to pray, share, and review their ministry. Finally, a new pastor is especially in need of some special attention from a priest responsible for ongoing formation as well as from a priest-pastor-mentor, who can offer more intense and frequent guidance in the first steps of assuming the responsibilities of pastor. These connections serve to ensure the accountability of priests in the process of ongoing formation, a critical element of the process at every stage.

Programs must necessarily vary from diocese to diocese because of varying resources. Some programmatic responses must necessarily be based in the diocese, such as the contact of new pastors with the bishop, other pastors, and a mentor. Other programs, such as initiation to requisite skills and knowledge, could be handled on a regional or even national basis. Particular cultural needs may be served by specific centers that can give an orientation to various pastoral situations, for example, parishioners who are Hispanic, African American, rural, migrant, or urban.

CONCLUSION

Parishes are complex realities. To be the pastor of a parish is a demanding task and responsibility, as well as a complicated, multifaceted ministry. At the same time, the case for complexity should not be overstated. Pastors do have a clear and single focus: to be present to and active in their parish communities as the abiding sacramental presence of Jesus Christ, the pastor of his flock. The ongoing formation of pastors, especially new pastors, aims to draw them to a unity or integrity of life by helping them to integrate who they are and what they do for the sake of the mission entrusted to them by the Good Shepherd.

D. Priests at Midlife: Ongoing Formation After a Certain Number of Years

INTRODUCTION

Modern developmental psychology has alerted us to the importance of midlife. Some speak of a "midlife crisis," as if it were possible to pinpoint an exact time of developmental transition. Others, perhaps more accurately, speak of midlife as a "season of life," stretched over a period of time. In any case, midlife is an important reality of human experience. Its issues, vulnerabilities, and possibilities are alive in us somewhere between the ages of forty to sixty. Priests, of course, are no exception to patterns of human development, including the season of midlife.

Although modern psychology has prompted us to consider midlife as a serious and important time, spiritual writers have long understood questions, challenges, and possibilities that touch the spiritual (and ministerial) journey after a certain number of years. A certain *taedium vitae*, a weariness of life, can set in; it is something that sets the stage for *acedia*, the noonday devil on the spiritual journey. Dante saw this time (*nel mezzo del cammin di nostra vita*) as an opportunity to re-examine life and re-establish one's direction.

Ongoing formation for priests in midlife is especially important in the United States. The demographic reality indicates that many priests are currently in this season of life, and how they respond to what midlife offers will be decisive for priestly ministry and life in this nation.

Documents of the universal Church strongly urge ongoing formation for priests in the context of midlife. *Pastores Dabo Vobis*, no. 77, does so with a heightened sense of the vulnerabilities and dangers that this time of life presents to priests: "They [priests] can face a number of risks, precisely because of their age, as for example, an exaggerated activism or a certain routine approach to the exercise of their ministry. As a result, the priest can be tempted to presume he can manage on his own, as if his own personal experience, which has seemed trustworthy to that point, needs no contact with anything or anyone else. Often enough, the older priest has a sort of interior fatigue which is dangerous. It can be a sign of resigned disillusionment in the face of difficulties and failures."

The *Directory on the Ministry and Life of Priests* also speaks of the urgency of ongoing formation for priests in midlife but from a sense of the positive possibilities that emerge from priestly ministry and life at this time: "After a certain number of years of ministry, priests acquire a solid experience and the great merit of having spent all their efforts in extending the Kingdom of God through daily work. This group of priests constitutes a great spiritual and pastoral resource. They need encouragement, genuine appreciation, a new deepening in all aspects of formation with the purpose of examining their actions, and a re-awakening of the motivation underlying the sacred ministry. They also need to reflect on pastoral methods in light of essentials, the communion among priests of the presbyterate, friendship with the Bishop, surmounting any sense of exhaustion, frustration and solitude and, finally, rediscovering the font of priestly spirituality" (no. 94).

The task ahead is to understand the event or season of midlife: its own tasks and challenges, the spiritual concerns linked to midlife, and possible programmatic responses to this period of life.

EVENT

It is important to note that a priest's midlife experience has many dimensions. These include physical, psychological, ministerial, and spiritual dimensions. Each of these will be considered in greater detail below.

It may also be helpful to identify a specific time in the larger midlife experience. One such moment provides a good focus for midlife concerns—the celebration of twenty-five years of priestly ministry. For many priests, this event coincides with their fiftieth year of life. (The current pattern of ordaining older candidates will shift these numbers, but for now the numbers hold.) Imagining priests who have served for twenty-five years and who will, God willing, serve for about another twenty-five locates us at the midpoint and may help to concretize what follows.

Physical

Men, including priests, at fifty become aware of physical changes that invite a new view of themselves. The vitality and ease of youth begins to pass. They are more aware of physical limitations and waning energy. Body changes make it clear that they are no longer young. In a youth-conscious culture such a realization strikes individuals with great force. Midlife is also a time when sickness or disability can readily become a part of the life journey. These physical changes both trigger and reflect a whole new set of psychological concerns.

Psychological

Physical diminishments raise a more general awareness of limitations in life. One's finitude becomes less theoretical and abstract, and more palpable and intensely felt. This new sense of limitation also presses to the truth of one's personal mortality—that life has an end and that more of life is behind than ahead. The decline in health and the deaths of a priest's parents reinforce his realization of mortality.

A sense of limitation and mortality, if not denied but faced directly and honestly, will inevitably lead to certain psychological processes. For example, one grieves the loss of what could have been and even what was. One re-evaluates personal commitments and investments and strives for greater authenticity. One considers the legacy that is to be left behind, what is yet to be generated. Finally, the disconnections triggered by the aging process re-surface concerns about intimacy and connection.

Ministerial and Pastoral

At midlife priests stand in a distinct ministerial situation. They may come to recognize what they have left undone and what may, for the rest of their lives, be "undoable." In effect, as they come to terms with the limits of their lives, they also do so with the limits of their ministry. Ecclesiastically, those in later midlife years may have "plateau-ed out." In other words, they probably have the position, responsibility, and recognition that will remain the same until they retire.

The accumulation of years of ministry also proves positive for priests at midlife. They are recognized as experienced and proven in their ability to do ministry. Often they receive greater ministerial and pastoral responsibility due to their proven competence and reliability. They function with an ease that stems from practice. In a more personal way, they may also experience a greater sense of wholeness or integration because they more easily draw together who they are and what they do, their identity and their service.

Ministry at midlife sets priests in a double line of responsibility. Because they are in the middle, they have responsibilities to the younger priests behind them: to welcome them, to encourage them, and to share ministry with them. They also have responsibilities to the older priests ahead of them: to maintain their legacy, to recognize their achievements, and to support them as they draw their ministry and life to a good conclusion. This double line of responsibility is not unlike that of other midlife people in the world, who are doubly responsible to their children and their parents. In the Church, the responsibility of midlife priests is shaped differently but is also directed to two generations, predecessors and successors.

Spiritual

The event or season of midlife sets an important context for priests' spiritual journey. Obviously, the issues raised by the season of midlife are not simply psychological. They resonate with faith concerns: limitation and mortality with the promise of eternal life, grief with detachment, authenticity with surrender and commitment, and intimacy with communion with God and others. Although for those who believe there can never be simply human concerns without a connection to faith and our gifted relationship with God, psychological issues need to be faced on their own terms and not be prematurely spiritualized.

Midlife for priests and other believers is also a season of epiphany. If one has stayed on the course of an intentional spiritual journey and if, at midlife, one stops and takes stock of what has been, inevitably the workings of grace become very manifest. That we have been transformed perhaps not fully and not perfectly, but truly and remarkably is made quite clear.

Midlife is life, a work still in progress. Spiritually, the journey continues, and midlife is also a season of renewal, of continuing the journey perhaps in some different, more intense, and more committed way.

TASKS AND CHALLENGES

The tasks and challenges of priests at midlife flow directly from the event or season of midlife as it is described above. The key dimensions of life affected by aging each need attention on their own terms. The overall goal is not to remedy or conquer midlife but to let it be a season of grace, a time of greater integration, another passage that leads to fuller transformation in the Lord and greater communion with him and with others. Although sensed limitations may spur priests to address the issues of midlife, it is midlife's opportunities and possibilities in faith that ultimately carry the greater weight and grace.

Physical

The care of oneself in midlife must include some way of addressing the physical dimensions of middle age. The task and challenge is to maintain health and to adapt appropriately to whatever physical limitations may already be present.

Psychological

The psychological tasks and challenges of midlife are obviously complex. One does not deal with a fresh sense of limitation, mortality, grief, re-evaluation of commitments, authenticity, generativity, and intimacy in a light or cavalier manner. In particular, questions about one's sexuality and celibate commitment can re-surface in pressing and challenging ways. The fundamental psychological task is to face the issues honestly and directly. Once they do this, priests grow in self understanding, which enables them to make more considered and realistic decisions

Ministerial and Pastoral

The ministerial and pastoral tasks for priests at midlife are multiple. They can best begin by identifying what their ministry *has been*. This initial move will allow them to confirm what is good and to continue in those directions. It will also enable them to see what needs adjustment and growth for the future. Logically, the next task is commitment to continue the good and to shore up what is weak or distorted. The task of commitment—if it is more than a notional or verbal commitment or if it is indeed an operative commitment—

includes developing the resources, supports, and connections that will enable the commitment to be lived realistically.

A final ministerial and pastoral task and challenge is to imagine and implement ways of responding to the twofold responsibility to the younger and older clergy, that is, by drawing the younger clergy more closely into the diocesan mission and by honoring and maintaining the legacy of those who have gone before.

Spiritual

In the midst of the complexities of midlife that bind together diminishment in some ways with expanded possibilities in others, the spiritual tasks and challenges are quite real and not unlike those of other times of life. Midlife priests experience the challenge of detachment, precisely in light of the changes and diminishments of midlife. At the same time, they also experience a call to the revitalization of their spiritual lives as they continue to progress on the spiritual journey both personally and in communion with the people they serve. Finally, priests face the challenge of holding fast to the confident center of their lives in Jesus Christ who is the great source of continuity in the midst of change.

The next section on spiritual concerns will elaborate on these very same issues.

SPIRITUAL CONCERNS: TEMPTATIONS, GRACES, DISCERNMENT
Temptations

The temptations that priests face at midlife are generally rooted in the wear and tear of the journey. With time, some inevitable weariness and regret develop. Temptations at midlife test the integrity of one's commitment and investments. They signal a choice either to move away from the journey as it has been or, with God's grace, to revitalize it.

Midlife temptations include a general pull to move off the course that has been set, to do something else before it is too late. Temptation may also leave the priest physically in place but affect him internally, for example, by drawing him into sadness, discouragement, or an isolated narrowness. Temptation can also incline priests to put a lens on life, for example, to view life and to act on it through disappointment and anger, perhaps even resentment. For every temptation that draws or pushes priests away from the path they have taken, there is a countervailing opportunity to stay the course and to do so even more intensively. It is a season of temptation but also of grace.

Graces

The fundamental grace offered priests at midlife is a triple gift in faith: (1) a deeper self-knowledge in faith, (2) a fuller self-acceptance in faith, and (3) a more generous self-gift in faith. These gifts are graces freely given, but they need to be claimed. God's fidelity to his gifts, especially his sacramental gifts, calls for a human response. God's graces are clearly connected with the lifelong process of integrating identity and service for the sake of mission.

Another grace evident at priests' midlife and related to the triple grace noted above is the opportunity to renegotiate their commitment and dedication. Missed opportunities, failures, and compromises in the first part of ministry need not have the last word. Midlife brings the offer and the grace of reconciliation, which can assume the form of re-commitment and re-dedication.

A final grace of midlife is life in communion that has grown over the years: the connections with the bishop, the presbyterate, the people served, and friends. The strong rush of emotion so often evident at jubilee Masses is due to the grace of holy connection, which has marked and continues to mark the ministry and lives of priests.

Discernment

Discernment at midlife has to do, as it does at other moments, with detecting the true movement of God in one's life. Clearly, the diminishments of midlife invite priests to consider how God is calling them to a deeper personal and apostolic detachment. At the same time, the opportunities for growth that also mark midlife invite a different kind of discernment: How is God calling me to a new responsiveness given my experience, the accumulated graces of these years, and the needs of the Church? Discernment grapples with fidelity and authenticity, with staying faithful and being true to oneself and to God's call.

If midlife requires a more economical use of time and energy, discernment sifts through the options available, not to sort out good from bad but to identify what might be more useful and in closer conformity with God's will. This is a three-point ministerial discernment that includes a sense of self, a sense of the Church's need, and a sense of God's direction.

Finally, discernment probes how to continue and deepen the communion in faith, hope, and love. This communion has given the priest at midlife a connected life and has made his celibate commitment truly generative. Again, the context of this discernment remains in God.

PROGRAMMATIC RESPONSES FOR PRIESTS AT MIDLIFE

In this instance as in others, exact programming must be locally based because it depends on particular needs and available resources. In a more general way, we can identify important elements of responding to priests at midlife, elements that ought to be incorporated in some form into the life of the local Church.

Sharing

If God moves not only in our individual lives but in each other in a corporate way, then we must listen not only to ourselves but to each other. The gathering of priests who are peers and experiencing midlife can be an invaluable resource. As they listen to each other, they can better understand their own situation and, at the same time, offer and receive support on the journey. Prayer groups, support groups, special retreats, and workshops can all contribute to the ongoing formation of midlife priests in effective ways.

Informing

As priests approach and live midlife, they need to *study* the phenomenon they are experiencing. Such study obviously ought to include questions surrounding the physical and psychological changes and challenges of midlife, but it must also be broad enough to include the spiritual and ministerial issues. Development, as we noted earlier, is not only the province of scientific psychology, it also has a venerable history in the spiritual tradition of the Church. Information and wisdom gathered from the tradition needs to be studied and assimilated.

Considering

A significant transition or season of transition in life, such as midlife itself, needs to be assimilated and absorbed. Solitude, quiet time, and space for reflection provide the context that makes assimilation and absorption possible. These may take shape more intensively in a retreat, or they may be included in some deliberate way in the patterns of daily life. In either case, the important value is giving priests an opportunity to consider, take hold, and draw into themselves in a deliberate fashion the different facets of the midlife experience.

Connecting

Midlife for priests is a particular opportunity, we noted, for exercising a double responsibility: to draw a younger generation into the mission and to honor and maintain the contribution of those who have gone before. That double responsibility needs some mechanism of establishing contact with the other surrounding generations. It can happen through the presbyteral council or groups of priestly fraternity, on the occasion of diocesan convocations, and at other opportunities as well. Specifics can vary, but the value needs to be maintained.

Another connection of great importance for priests at midlife is with their bishop. Given their experience and their future ministry in the diocese, these priests form an invaluable segment of the presbyterate for the bishop of the local Church. For the sake of the mission, it is important that connections with the bishop be deepened.

Utilizing Personal Resources and Programs

Under the category of personal resources and programs are the multiple ways that priests can and should seek counsel as individuals. They need, for example, to care for themselves physically and medically, and, therefore, they need good medical consultation.

Psychological assistance is a more delicate matter because it still curiously carries with it, in certain quarters, associations with mental deterioration. In fact, a series of psychological consultations in the course of midlife can be very useful in sorting out cognitive issues, such as the most effective path to learning in midlife; emotional issues, such as the appropriate responses to sensed limitations; and value issues, such as the most effective way of revitalizing commitments.

Midlife for priests can also mean that some personal planning is in order. A senior priest-mentor can be helpful as one makes plans concerning physical needs, finance, ministerial investments, and retirement.

Finally, on a personal level, there is a deep need for a spiritual director/confessor. Everything that has been said about midlife only makes final sense in the perspective of faith. Only when midlife is seen in the narrative of God's grace that stretches across our lives from birth to death does it fill out with meaning. A spiritual director can help guide this extraordinarily important appropriation of life events in faith. The use of these resources and programs correspond to a special kind of accountability that belongs to priests at midlife. In their accountability to God and their people, they seek to continue their service in ever more effective ways.

E. Priests Growing in Wisdom and Grace: Ongoing Formation and Senior Clergy

INTRODUCTION

Recent studies and reflections on aging speak of "the third age," the period that spans from ages sixty-five to ninety-five and, sometimes, beyond that. That more people live longer and continue to lead active lives is the result of developments in medicine and other benefits associated with living today in the United States.

Priests are part of the graying of America. As they age, they still have a need for ongoing formation, although tailored to their specific season of life.

Both *Pastores Dabo Vobis* (no. 77) and the *Directory on the Ministry and Life of Priests* (no. 95) strongly urge ongoing formation for priests of advanced age. Both documents underscore a double purpose in such formation. It must serve to support priests as they face the challenges that this time of life offers, but must also encourage priests to continue to make their unique and irreplaceable contribution to the Church and its mission, again on the basis of their experience and the special season of their life.

Any introduction to the ongoing formation of senior clergy ought to proceed modestly. Extended life expectancies and a sustained high quality of life into advanced age are new phenomena. In a real sense, they provide a new challenge to spiritual formation in Christian history. For now, much must be tentative. For example, we do not have a clear set of distinctions within the general class of senior clergy. Surely, within a group that spans thirty years a number of distinctions ought to be made, but these are not yet available to us. Terms such as "retirement" need to be freshly understood both in secular and religious worlds. Older persons, including priests, continue to be who they have been, and often they continue to maintain a level of activity at least equal to the time prior to their "retirement."

Although we are limited in our understanding of the new phenomenon of aging, touchstones of human, spiritual, and priestly formation can still be of help. The issue of integrating identity and function, for example, is perennial, although it has a particular shape for senior clergy. One must also face the prospect of decline and death in the advanced years, since longevity and continued health are relative, not absolute realities, in the aging process. Faith speaks to such concerns. Formation attends to them.

In the sections that follow, we will consider the event or, better, the season of priests' advanced years: the tasks and challenges that face priests during that time, the spiritual concerns they might have, and some of the possible programmatic responses to their ongoing formation.

EVENT
Senior clergy experience the aging process in continuity with the dynamics of midlife: some physical decline, psychological issues related to shifts in living and working, pastoral and ministerial readjustments based on different energy levels and accumulated experience, and spiritual possibilities unfolding in the journey of faith.

A distinctive moment and experience for senior clergy is "retirement." If "retirement" in priesthood is seen as exactly parallel to the secular sense of retirement—for example, as a complete withdrawal from activities and responsibilities that had marked one's active work life—then this may be a misnomer.

Priests are not simply functionaries, workers, or professionals. Who they are sacramentally, their way of being, is as crucial, if not more so, than their particular functioning. In retirement they do not cease *to be* priests, even if there is a shift in what they *do* as priests or in the specific responsibilities they *have* as priests. The event of retirement for priests, then, marks not a radical change of life or vocation but a realignment of activity and responsibility that can have significant human and spiritual impact.

The season of advanced age for clergy raises a set of three questions about the future: (1) What do I do with the time remaining to me in this life? (2) In what way do I want to contribute to the future of the Church? (3) How shall I move toward eternal life? In technical terms, these questions reflect concerns that are existential, generative, and eschatological. They demonstrate a richness and texture that the future assumes in the season of advanced age for priests. They belie the conceptions of advanced age as the end of life in the popular culture.

TASKS AND CHALLENGES

Senior priests obviously face the challenge of increasing physical limitations that are a natural part of the aging process or the consequences of illness. Psychological issues connected with greater physical limitation also present a challenge. Senior priests need to confront the challenges and address them in whatever way is appropriate. Ordinarily, these are not challenges that one can confront alone. Generally some counsel is necessary, whether medical, psychological, or social.

The task of integration presses senior priests with great urgency. It is very important that they revisit in this season of their life the question of integrating who they are and what they do for the sake of mission—their identity linked to their service for the purpose of the Gospel. The urgency derives from the fact that *who they are* in this time of their priesthood takes clearer precedence over *what they do*.

A task and challenge that marks the entire Christian life is participating in the dying and rising of Jesus Christ, sharing in his paschal mystery. For senior priests for whom the prospect of physical death is a more immediate possibility, preparing to die in the Lord so that they can rise with him is singularly important. This preparation entails sealing one's life with an Amen to God and to God's will. It also means practiced detachment from what one has and from what one has accomplished. For when we go to God, we go simply as who we are, not with anything we have or have done. The spiritual growth implicit in this process of preparation is an ever-greater dependence on God.

A final and important task and challenge is to contribute to the life and mission of the Church. Obviously, the path of contribution needs to fit the possibilities and the particular gifts of senior clergy. Their contribution, however, is real and, indeed, decisive for the good of the Church. For example, their witness and explicit affirmation of the value of priestly ministry and commitment after many years is an extraordinarily strong and energizing force in the Church, a force that encourages vocations and perseverance among those already ordained. The intercessory prayer of senior clergy is a priestly service of incalculable value in the Church. Their collective wisdom generously shared is their great gift and legacy to a younger generation.

SPIRITUAL CONCERNS: TEMPTATIONS, GRACES, DISCERNMENT

The spirituality of advanced age is yet to be developed. Relatively short life expectancies, until this moment in history, precluded much sustained reflection on the topic. Hints are given in the tradition. The Bible speaks of older people falling into foolishness like Saul or, more positively, of their great vocation to wait, watch, and proclaim the Messiah like Simeon and Anna. It is the clear responsibility of our time to observe the spiritual journeys of older people carefully and to make note of patterns that will serve future generations. Even with significant limits of our understanding, there are some things that we can confidently affirm about the spiritual journeys of senior priests.

Temptations

In one sense, our personal sets of temptations have an amazing staying power. Not uncommonly, what threatened to derail our spiritual journey at twenty re-asserts itself at fifty, sixty, or seventy. Still there is a specificity about spiritual testing in advanced age. It has to do with our accounting for the past and our prospects for the future.

Senior priests gather a lifetime of ministry and can be tempted to wonder whether their efforts made a difference, whether what they did was worthwhile, whether what remains undone eclipses the little that was accomplished. This is the temptation to despair the past, and one can either succumb to it by falling into a deep sadness or resist it by surrendering ultimate responsibility to God where it belongs.

Senior priests also find themselves tempted about their prospects for the future or, more precisely, the lack of prospects for the future. As they look ahead, they may see the possibility of debilitating illness accompanied by increasing and humiliating dependency. Faith in eternal life may itself be tested as death looms large on the horizon, and a void seems more likely than a fullness. To succumb to temptations about the future means to lose hope, to despair. To resist that temptation, however, may bring one to a purified faith, a single trust, and a sustained "yes" to God in the face of seemingly pervasive negativity.

Graces

The graces, like the temptations, stretch across a lifetime. The specific graces of this season of life include a sense of wisdom and insight, the fruit of patiently considered and prayerfully received experience.

Another grace is linked with coming to the conclusion of life. It is the gift of focus, of grasping what really matters, of knowing what are peripheral details and what or who is at the center.

A final grace is hope. This is, of course, to be distinguished from wishful thinking that results from our own fanciful constructions of life. The grace or gift of hope is God's gift, and its cost is loving trust in the giver. The last phase of physical life sharpens the gift of hope and intensifies its cost.

Discernment

Discernment, as we have already noted, is the discovery of a God-given direction in our lives. We sort out the various movements of our heads and hearts. In the movements, God speaks. Discernment invites us to listen carefully and to notice attentively.

Senior priests bring a series of questions to the discernment process: How ought I to detach myself from my past, from my work, from the old routines of life? What should I do with the time and energy allotted to me? How can I be present and available to the community of faith that needs and wants me? How can I give effective witness to the mercies of God that have marked my life? How can I become more pliant to the will of God as God calls me to the complete gift of myself?

Issues surrounding celibacy and sexuality for senior clergy are generally glossed over, but there are important spiritual prospects here that need consideration and discernment. As celibates draw their lives to a conclusion, there is a poignancy about doing so alone and without physical progeny. The spiritual meaning of celibacy as a loving and life-giving way of life needs to be personally re-appropriated by senior priests. This means a discernment process that seeks to detect how God has moved in them and through them as they have lived out their dedication. They must somehow come to hear the promise made to another old man, Abraham: "I am making you the father of a host of nations. I will render you exceedingly fertile; I will make nations of you" (Gn 17:5-6). This discernment process reflects the way that this season of life, no less than every other, carried with it a significant dimension of accountability to God, the Church, and the people served.

PROGRAMMATIC RESPONSES FOR SENIOR CLERGY

A proliferation of programs for senior clergy would not be helpful. The *Directory on the Ministry and Life of Priests* expresses it in this way: "The elderly priests or those advanced in years who merit special consideration, enter in the vital circle of ongoing formation, not so much regarding thorough study and discussion of cultural subjects, but rather 'the calm and reassuring confirmation of the part which they are still called to play in the presbyterate'" (no. 95; cf. PDV, no. 77). Structures and structured responses to senior clergy need to confirm them in their particular life and vocational situation.

Lecture and workshop opportunities to study and understand the human and spiritual dynamics of the aging process can be helpful. Personal and group counseling and assistance in making plans for living, serving as priest, and giving witness to the Church can also be useful.

A deepened spiritual renewal that touches the faith meaning of their lives is an especially important task for senior priests. It can be addressed through retreats, days of renewal, and individualized spiritual direction.

A Catholic sense of sacramentality and community would also encourage public celebrations of senior priests. This acknowledgment in a context of grateful prayer enables them to give witness to the community at large. Other gatherings of priests and laity ought to make special provision for "the elders among them," so that their wisdom and grace can be acknowledged and more generously shared.

A consciousness raising in the Church concerning senior priests can benefit the entire Church. The bishop, other priests, friends and family of senior priests, and young people need to take conscious hold of the presence and gifts of senior clergy. In this way, theirs will never be a forgotten grace in the Church.

Part Three

THE ONGOING FORMATION OF AN ENTIRE PRESBYTERATE

A. Introduction

To pursue the ongoing formation not simply of priests but of a presbyterate as a whole brings us to new territory. The Church continues to deepen her understanding of priestly ministry and life that emerged in the Second Vatican Council; namely, priests are not priests simply one by one, but they are priests and serve the mission of the Church in a presbyterate in union with the bishop. The corporate sense of priestly identity and mission, although not fully developed even in official documents, is clearly emerging as an important direction for the future.

Pastores Dabo Vobis, no. 74, offers a rich synthesis of the origins, identity, and mission of presbyterates. It can serve as a solid foundation for considering the ongoing formation of a presbyterate. It reads as follows:

> Within the ecclesial communion, the priest is called in particular to *grow*, thanks to his ongoing formation, *in and with his own presbyterate in union with his Bishop*. The presbyterate, in the fullness of its truth, is a *mysterium*: it is in fact a supernatural reality because it is rooted in the Sacrament of Holy Orders. This is its source and origin. This is its "place" of birth and of its growth. Indeed, "priests by means of the Sacrament of Orders are tied with a personal and indissoluble bond to Christ the one priest. The Sacrament of Holy Orders is conferred upon each of them as individuals, but they are inserted into the communion of the presbyterate united with the Bishop (*Lumen Gentium*, 28; *Presbyterorum Ordinis*, 7 and 8)" (*Propositio* 34).

This sacramental origin is reflected and continued in the sphere of priestly ministry: from *mysterium* to *ministerium*. "Unity among the priests with the

Bishop and among themselves is not something added from the outside to the nature of their service, but expresses its essence inasmuch as it is the care of Christ the priest for the People gathered in the unity of the Blessed Trinity" (*Propositio* 34). This unity among priests, lived in a spirit of pastoral charity, makes priests witnesses of Jesus Christ, who prayed to the Father "that they may all be one" (Jn 17:21).

The *formation* of a presbyterate is given by God sacramentally. The *ongoing formation* of a presbyterate is the deliberate cultivation of the unity of the priests and their bishop, a unity that responds to God's grace and the mission entrusted to them. The ongoing formation of presbyterates has a three-fold purpose intimated in *Pastores Dabo Vobis* that underscores its urgency and importance.

MISSIONARY AND MINISTERIAL PURPOSE
The ongoing formation of a presbyterate aims to forge a *collective sense of study and prayer* among the priests of the presbyterate for the sake of their service to the people of God entrusted to their care. Common prayer and study enable the diverse members of a presbyterate to have a common language and mind about the mission they serve through their ministry, as well as a common heart committed and attached to the heart of Jesus Christ, High Priest. A unified presbyterate can move "from *mysterium* to *ministerium*" (PDV, no. 74).

PURPOSE OF PROMOTING PASTORAL CHARITY
The ongoing formation of a presbyterate's unity cultivates the bonds of *fraternal connection, support, and challenge*. This is the "unity among priests, lived in a spirit of pastoral charity" (PDV, no. 74). Far from being a fraternity closed in on itself, a truly unified presbyterate dynamically redirects itself outward in pastoral charity, as priests engage in "uniting themselves with Christ in the recognition of the Father's will and in the gift of themselves to the flock entrusted to them" (PO, no. 14). In this way, they are "adopting the role of the good shepherd" (ibid.). So, the formation of a presbyterate in its unity and fraternity aims, ultimately, to promote a more intense pastoral charity.

SACRAMENTAL PURPOSE
The ongoing formation of a presbyterate's unity makes the very presbyterate *a more transparent sacramental sign*. "This unity among priests . . . makes [them]

witnesses of Jesus Christ, who prayed to the Father 'that they may all be one'" (PDV, no. 74). The unity of the presbyterate is a sacramental sign in the Church and for the world of humanity's calling to be drawn into the very life of the Holy Trinity. Jesus prays for unity among his disciples and especially those who will have the apostolic mission. He prays for their participation in *Trinitarian* unity: "that they may all be one, as you, Father, are in me and I in you, that they also may be in us" (Jn 17:21). And the very purpose of that unity is a sacramental one, in the order of efficacious signs, to draw others into faith: "that the world may believe that you sent me" (Jn 17:21).

It is clear that the ongoing formation of presbyterates is significant for the vitality of the Church's mission. It is also clear that the formation of presbyterates centers on cultivating their unity. The three sections that follow will address (1) divisions as blocks to unity in presbyterates, (2) the biblical and ecclesial foundations of presbyteral unity, and (3) some practical suggestions for the ongoing formation of presbyterates.

B. Facing Divisions and Their Consequences

If presbyteral unity is the goal of the ongoing formation of presbyterates, then the divisions that impede and imperil that unity must be accurately identified and honestly faced. The consequences of divisions must also receive attention. These considerations establish a *via negativa* that prepares a way for the more constructive approaches to the formation of presbyterates.

FACTORS THAT CAN CONTRIBUTE TO DIVISIONS IN PRESBYTERATES
The root experience of sin is inner division. *Homo in seipso divisus est.* "The human person is divided in himself or herself" (GS, no. 10). Divisions cause separations and alienation. The movement of redemption in salvation history is always directed toward the restoration of unity with God and with one another —reconciliation.

On the way to healing and transformation, it is important to identify factors that contribute to division. Once named they can be addressed. This is true for presbyterates. Below are some factors that contribute to the divisions within presbyterates.

Competition

As men ministering in an American cultural context, preists, like other men, find themselves socialized into particular ways of relating and moving through life. Competition and comparison form a significant pattern of socialization evident in contemporary American culture that shapes the way males relate to other boys and men. This competition and comparison can easily foster division.

Different Formational Generations in a Presbyterate

A single presbyterate can easily contain at least four different "formational generations," that is, priests formed in a particular personal, spiritual, and ministerial pattern. Priests from these generations must work side by side but often uneasily and sometimes with apparent divisions. The reference point for different formational generations is the Second Vatican Council, and the generations (that should not be conceived too rigidly) are pre-Vatican Council, pre-and-post Vatican Council, post-Vatican Council, and a new emergent formational generation. These formational generations also reflect the shifts that have occurred in American culture over the past fifty years.

Invidia Clericalis with a Modern Touch

Clerical envy has always been with us (cf. Jn 21:20-22). In our contemporary situation, it is aggravated by the lack of a sense of what it means to advance as a priest. In a hierarchical structure (which parallels business, the military, or government/politics), one might assume that advancement would be correlative to higher rank, greater responsibility, or a bigger paycheck. In fact, making progress as a priest cannot be correlated with any of these signs or symbols of advancement. Authentic progress in priestly ministry and life means *being* a more transparent sacramental sign and *doing* better the tasks of priestly ministry. When, however, there is a lack of clarity about advancement or its symbols, priests will react or respond to what they *think* are the presence of such signs in others and the lack in themselves. This is a fertile ground for breeding divisions.

The Bishop's Support of Presbyteral Unity

A bishop has many responsibilities, and many things claim his attention. Presbyteral unity may not seem to be as pressing, for example, as dealing with individual priests who are problematic, with the distribution and assignment of clergy, or with the recruitment of new candidates. Working for presbyteral unity can slip to a lower end of a list of priorities. In fact, its neglect favors divisions and, ultimately, a number of attendant problems in a diocese.

Varied Backgrounds of Those Entering the Presbyterate
Vocations to the priesthood in the past followed a predictable pattern. Young men entered the seminary at an early age, went through the process together, and were ordained at about the age of twenty-five or twenty-six. Candidates now come into the seminary program at different points and with varying life and work experiences. Although their diversity can be enriching, it makes unity and cohesiveness in the presbyterate more challenging and can, in fact, lead to divisions.

Different Theologies and Spiritualities
Although faith is one, it can take a number of expressions in theological forms that may be more or less adequate to the task. The current state of theological pluralism can fracture the ability of priests to talk to each other in a common theological language. This, of course, can contribute to divisions among them. Similarly, differences in spiritualities—the practice of faith—can impede a sense of unity.

Differences of Language, Culture, and Place of Origin
We have never ceased to be an immigrant country, and this fact has had and continues to have an impact on the Church. Priests come into presbyterates with different racial, cultural, and language backgrounds. Frequently, they have not been born in the United States. Although these differences can be enriching, frequently they cause distancing in presbyterates and create dividing lines drawn by language and culture.

CONSEQUENCES OF DIVISIONS IN PRESBYTERATES
Divisions in presbyterates have many significant consequences. They lead, for example, to diminished effectiveness in priests' ability to serve God and his people by undermining the utilization of resources in a presbyterate to address pressing issues. Another consequence follows when divisions are public; they constitute an anti-sign for the community of faith. Divisions in presbyterates discourage those who might feel called to priesthood. Finally, divisions can shift the ministerial focus of priests from a wide-ranging, diocesan perspective

to a narrow, localized emphasis on one's own parish with a resultant parochialism or congregationalism.

C. The Nature of Presbyteral Unity: Biblical and Ecclesial Foundations

The ongoing formation of a presbyterate, as we have noted initially and through a *via negativa* in the examination of divisions, has to do with cultivating the unity of the presbyterate. What needs further determination is the nature of that unity.

Before examining the biblical and ecclesial understandings of unity that can be helpful to grasp the nature of presbyteral unity, it can be useful to eliminate what presbyteral unity *is not*. Presbyteral unity, for example, is obviously not based on blood relationships. Nor is it dependent on friendship or even like-mindedness. Although some would assert that it means greater efficiency in serving the Church and the world, it does not essentially serve a functional purpose. It does not mean that everyone must be the same. And, of course, presbyteral unity is never legitimately anchored into an attitude of superiority or chauvinism, which is in fact clericalism.

BIBLICAL WITNESS

The Bible, especially the New Testament, can offer perspectives that ground the reality of presbyteral unity in God's design. The Johannine perspective cites the petition of Jesus "that they may all be one, as you, Father, are in me and I in you, that they also may be in us, that the world may believe that you sent me" (Jn 17:21). Presbyteral unity, in this perspective, is linked to the unity of the Father and Son in the Holy Spirit from which it draws its life and has, as its purpose, the effective witness and proclamation of the truth of Jesus Christ sent by the Father for the salvation of the world.

In the Pauline corpus, unity in ministry—which can easily be translated into a presbyteral context—is viewed as a reality that is both christological and pneumatological. For example, in the first chapter of 1 Corinthians, Paul demonstrates how diverse ministry exercised by different people leads us back to a center in Christ, who is the unifying principle of all service: "Each of you is saying, 'I belong to Paul,' or, 'I belong to Apollos,' or, 'I belong to Kephas,' or, 'I belong to Christ.' Is Christ divided? Was Paul crucified for you? Or were you baptized in the name of Paul?" (1:12-13).

Elsewhere in the Pauline corpus, one finds a pneumatological basis for unity in ministry. For example, in the fourth chapter of the letter to the Ephesians: "[Strive] to preserve the unity of the spirit through the bond of peace: one body and one Spirit, as you were also called to the one hope of your call" (Eph 4:3-4).

The biblical witness, when applied to the question of the nature of presbyteral unity, gives it shape and substance, first by differentiating it from a product of human effort and then by identifying it with a grace that is trinitarian, christological, and pneumatological.

DOCUMENTS OF THE CHURCH

Three passages from Pope John Paul II's apostolic exhortation *Pastores Dabo Vobis*, in part cited earlier, provide a fuller elaboration of the formative nature of presbyteral unity.

Number 17 summarizes teaching from Vatican II and offers this simple yet challenging statement: "The ordained ministry has a radical *'communitarian form'* and can only be carried out as 'a collective work.'" This truly is the teaching of the Second Vatican Council abundantly evident in *Presbyterorum Ordinis*, which so emphasizes the communitarian-collective dimension of priestly ministry that it quite deliberately avoids any reference to "priest" in the singular form. From start to finish, the decree only speaks of "priests."

Number 74 of *Pastores Dabo Vobis*, which has already been cited, identifies priestly sacramental existence as essentially and intrinsically linked to a life lived in unity among priests themselves and with their bishop. The text reads, "Unity among the priests with the Bishop and among themselves is not something added from the outside to the nature of their service, but expresses its essence inasmuch as it is the care of Christ the priest for the People gathered in the unity of the Blessed Trinity." These words speak of the *sacramental* value of living presbyteral unity. Such unity lived out becomes an effective or efficacious sign of the presence of Christ caring for his people and leading them into the unity of the Trinity.

Finally, number 12 elaborates the basis for presbyteral unity by linking it to the heart of the Church's mission and humanity's trinitarian destiny: "The nature and mission of the ministerial priesthood cannot be defined except through this multiple and rich interconnection of relationships which arise from the Blessed Trinity and are prolonged in the communion of the Church, as a sign and instrument of Christ, of communion with God and of the unity of all humanity."

D. Practical Possibilities for the Formation of a Presbyterate

After understanding the importance of presbyteral unity and formation, the divisions that militate against it, and the biblical and ecclesial traditions that highlight its essential nature, the next step is to identify practical possibilities to support and nurture it.

PRAYING TOGETHER
Praying together informally and in more formal, ritualized contexts contributes to the formation of a presbyterate. Liturgical celebrations, such as concelebrated Eucharist with the bishop and the common praying of the Liturgy of the Hours, are very contributory to unity. Prayer together may also take more extended forms, such as retreats, days of renewal, and days of sanctification.

In a more general way, the forging of a common consciousness in a presbyterate that begins to see itself as a community of intercession, pleading especially for the people entrusted to its care, is a strong and formative movement.

STUDYING TOGETHER
When a presbyterate comes together to study, especially the more urgent pastoral questions that affect the lives of the people it serves, it shares communion in wisdom. It also develops a common vocabulary, pools the intellectual

resources of its individual priests, and takes common responsibility for the dilemmas that touch the lives of countless people.

Study together can happen through study weeks or days, or in the course of convocations. Study together can also be carried out in small groups that meet regularly.

PLANNING TOGETHER

When the presbyterate in communion with the bishop identifies the needs of the local church and develops strategies of response, it shares in a communion of mission. This can happen through the presbyteral council, at-large consultations with the presbyterate, a diocesan synodal process, or, even more locally, in vicariates and deaneries. The dynamics are simple but extraordinary: to come together, to listen to God, to listen to the needs of the people, to listen to the inner promptings of the Holy Spirit, to be in dialogue with one another and with Christ's faithful people, to be in spiritual conversation, and to make decisions that take into account how the word will be proclaimed, the mysteries of Christ will be celebrated, and the mission of the Church will be furthered.

INFORMAL CONTACT

The fraternal bonds of a presbyterate are forged and deepened not only in the context of prayer and work done together but also through the informal contact that priests in a presbyterate have with one another. These become occasions of mutual recognition and support and, on occasion, of healthy challenge.

Given the pace of parish life today and time demands that are made on priests, a kind of planned spontaneity may be the only way that such informal contact can be made. It does, however, seem worth the effort because it is an essential ingredient of presbyteral unity and formation.

CREATIVE LINKING

The examination of divisions in presbyterates leads to a practical conclusion about the necessity of deliberately linking priests across different categories. Whether in the process of prayer, study, planning, or informal contact, it is formationally necessary to establish connections in different directions of the presbyterate. For example, it is important to link priests across generational lines, theological persuasions, ethnicity, and differences in places of origin. Although almost everyone in a presbyterate would acknowledge the value of such linking across potential divides, it will not happen spontaneously. It needs explicit commitment on the part of the priests and some creative and deliberate mechanisms of implementation.

SIGNIFICANT PERSONS IN THE PRESBYTERATE

The formation of the presbyterate in its unity is the responsibility of all its members. At the same time, individuals in the presbyterate have a particular responsibility for holding the values of presbyteral formation before all the priests. In this way, they encourage and support ongoing formation of the presbyterate.

The bishop certainly has this position and responsibility. He is both a sign and instrument of unity for his presbyterate. One significant way that he fulfills his responsibility is by regularly holding the mission of the local church and the presbyterate before the priests. He redirects the presbyterate to its singular purpose.

The presbyteral council represents the presbyterate and assists the bishop in his governance of the diocese. As such, it plays an important role in fostering the unity of the presbyterate and in promoting the ongoing formation of priests.

The director of ongoing formation offers support and program possibilities to the priests individually and to the presbyterate at large. He can help the priests translate their responsibility to pray together, to study together, and to plan together into practical possibilities.

Similarly, vicars and deans have a position and perspective that enables them to understand the challenges that a presbyterate faces. They can contribute to a collective or corporate awareness of the challenges and graces available to the presbyterate.

The individuals and groups named thus far represent official structures in the diocese and the presbyterate. Still others function in an unofficial but highly significant way. For example, senior clergy as a body are often the presbyteral memory of the diocese. They can contribute greatly to the ongoing formation of the presbyterate by recalling and reminding the priests of their collective history and sense of mission. Their own witness of faithful service enliven the presbyterate with a spirit of perseverance. Their wisdom and accumulated experience provide invaluable resources.

Other "unofficial" leaders in the presbyterate can be very instrumental in its formation. For example, the leaders of language or ethnic groups within a presbyterate can contribute to the integration and unification of a presbyterate composed of many different priests. The "spiritual fathers" in a presbyterate can continue to encourage and support the journey of presbyteral formation.

E. Conclusion

The formation of a presbyterate is a task of great importance. It begins with God who sacramentally establishes or forms a presbyterate. It continues in the free response to this great grace by the priests who are assembled with their bishop. The ongoing formation of a presbyterate has a focus in cultivating and nurturing the unity of the presbyterate. That unity not only provides a source of effective apostolic ministry in consort, but it also becomes an effective sign of God's plan of unity for the Church and for all humanity. The basis for the formation of a presbyterate in the Bible and the teachings of the Church are essential to keep presbyterates focused on the authentic foundations and destiny of their unity. It is also important, however, that the practical possibilities for cultivating the unity and formation of a presbyterate be clear.

Appendix

DOCTRINAL UNDERSTANDING OF THE MINISTERIAL PRIESTHOOD

Excerpted from the National Conference of Catholic Bishops'
Program for Priestly Formation (1992)

A. Trinitarian Source

"The priest's identity . . . like every Christian identity, has it source in the Blessed Trinity."[1] "The communion of Christians with Jesus has the communion of God as Trinity, namely, the unity of the Son to the Father in the gift of the Holy Spirit, as its model and source, and is itself the means to achieve this communion: United to the Son in the Spirit's bond of love, Christians are united to the Father."[2]

B. Jesus Christ, the Perfect High Priest

In the fullness of time, God sent the Eternal Word into the world and into the midst of human history. "For God so loved the world that he gave his only Son that whoever believes in him should not perish but have eternal life."[3] Jesus Christ, "whom the Father sanctified and sent into the world,"[4] proclaimed the good news of God's reconciliation with the human family. Confirmed by word and deed, his preaching reached its summit in the paschal mystery, the supreme manifestation of the Father's love.

"On the cross, Jesus showed himself to the greatest possible extent to be the good shepherd who laid down his life for his sheep." Surpassing "all the ritual priesthood and holocausts of the Old Testament," Christ exercised a supreme and unique priesthood.[5] As perfect victim and ideal priest, he bore the sins of all and entered the heavenly sanctuary.[6] "Rising from the dead and being made Lord (cf. Phil 2:9-11), he reconciled us to God; and he laid the foundation of the people of the new covenant, which is the Church."[7]

C. A Royal Priesthood

The Second Vatican Council has described the Church as "the people of God, the body of Christ, the bride of Christ, the temple of the Holy Spirit, the family of God."[8] In different ways, these images "bring to light the reality of the Church as a communion with its inseparable dimensions: the communion of each Christian with Christ and the communion of all Christians with one another."[9] By communicating his Spirit, Christ continually forms and reforms those who become his brothers and sisters in baptism. "As all the members of the human body, though they are many, form one body, so also are the faithful in Christ."[10] Christ the eternal high priest shares with his body, the Church, the anointing that he himself received.[11] Through the waters of baptism and by the power of the Holy Spirit, the faithful are formed into a royal priesthood and joined to Christ, becoming sharers in a common vocation to holiness and a mission to evangelize the world.[12]

D. Priesthood in the Person of Christ, Head and Shepherd of the Church

"For the sake of this universal priesthood of the New Covenant Jesus gathered disciples during his earthly mission" (cf. Lk 10:1-12),[13] "to carry out publicly in the church a priestly ministry."[14] They were to minister in a special way to those with whom they were united in the body of Christ, a body in which "all members have not the same function."[15] Thus while all the baptized participate in the priesthood of Christ, some are called and ordained to minister to all of the faithful. In the sacrament of orders, priests are especially configured to Christ to act in his person as head and pastor of the Church and in the name of the whole people of God.[16] Priests are ministers who receive their sacred authority from Christ through the Church.

Conferred in the sacrament of orders, "the priesthood, along with the word of God and the sacramental signs which it serves, belong to the constitutive elements of the Church."[17] Although the reality of priestly ministry emanated from Christ, its differentiation and precise naming occurred in successive generations of the Christian community under the guidance of the Holy Spirit.

The figure of the good shepherd who calls each by name and lays down his life for his flock stands as a sign of that special configuration to Christ that belongs to priests by virtue of the sacrament of orders.

"Though they differ essentially and not only in degree, the common priesthood of the faithful and the ministerial or hierarchical priesthood are nonetheless ordered one to another; each in its own proper way shares in the one priesthood of Christ. The ministerial priest, by the sacred power that he has, forms and rules the priestly people; in the person of Christ, he effects the eucharistic sacrifice and offers it to God in the name of all the people. The faithful indeed, by virtue of their royal priesthood, participate in the offering of the Eucharist. They exercise that priesthood, too, by the reception of the sacraments, prayer and thanksgiving, the witness of a holy life, abnegation and active charity."[18] "The ministry of the priest is entirely on behalf of the Church; it aims at promoting the exercise of the common priesthood of the entire people of God."[19]

E. To Teach, to Sanctify, and to Lead

Configured to Christ, head of the Church, and intimately united as co-workers of the bishops, priests are commissioned in a unique way to continue Christ's mission as prophet, priest, and king.[20] Their primary duty is to proclaim the Gospel to the whole world by word and deed. This mission extends to all people, even those for whom the Gospel has ceased to be a message of hope or a challenge to right action.[21] The preaching of the Gospel finds its source and culmination in the Eucharist. Priests exercise the office of sanctifying the Christian people in the celebration of the sacraments of the Church. As members of the one presbyterate gathered around the bishop, priests serve to unite the local church in one great act of worship of the Father. Finally, priests exercise the office of shepherd, because of the "specific ontological bond which unites the priesthood to Christ the high priest and good shepherd."[22] Called to gather together the family of Christ, priests act with a spiritual authority that enables them to lead the people of God along right paths.[23] In these and similar ways, priests are servants of Christ present in the Church as mystery, actuating Christ's presence in the sacraments; as communion, building up the body of Christ; and as mission, heralding the Gospel.[24]

The anointing of the Holy Spirit in the sacrament of orders is conferred through the hands of a bishop, thereby constituting priests into the presbyterate of a local church either as diocesan priests or as members of a religious community. They also become part of a worldwide sacramental order of priests.[25] "Because it is joined with the episcopal order the office of priests shares in the authority by which Christ himself builds up and sanctifies and rules his body. Hence the priesthood of priests, while presupposing the sacraments of initiation, is nevertheless conferred by its own particular sacrament. Through that sacrament priests, by the anointing of the Holy Spirit, are signed with a special character and so are configured to Christ the priest in such a way that they are able to act in the person of Christ the head."[26] Ordained priests remain sacramentally related to Christ and to his Church for life with a character that perdures into eternity.

Sharing in the one priesthood of Christ, priests are called to an enduring sacramental relation to their bishop.[27] This union is expressed not only in the action by which priests are ordained but also in daily Eucharist and other liturgical actions. Although committed to a great diversity of individual ministries, priests are united in the common goal of building up the body of Christ through ordained priestly service.

F. Ministerial Priesthood in a Religious Community

Not all priests are ordained directly to the service of a local church.[28] God has blessed the Church with religious communities that take their inspiration from the example of Christ as the source of the evangelical counsels of poverty, chastity, and obedience. From the God-given seed of the counsels, a variety of forms of religious life has sprung up for the growth of the body of Christ and for the progress in holiness of its members.[29]

The ministerial priesthood experienced and exercised in religious life, although not different in essence from diocesan priesthood, finds its expression in a setting that reflects the charism of the religious community. The reality of the priesthood is the same for all who are ordained, yet the lived expression of sacred orders will reflect the diocesan or religious context of priesthood.

At the same time, the exercise of the priesthood relates religious priests to the bishop who is head of the local church where they exercise priestly ministry. Although religious priests, canonically and spiritually, enjoy a primary relationship with their religious ordinary, they also have an ecclesiological and pastoral relationship to the bishop and the presbyterate of the diocese in which they serve.

G. Pastoral Leadership in the Community of Faith

Priests provide pastoral leadership in the community of faith. From the waters of baptism and the outpouring of the Holy Spirit, priests and laity share a sacramental origin and a common purpose as disciples of Christ. These bonds imply a continuing relationship of collaboration and mutual respect. The competence, love, and gifts of the laity complement and support the ministry of priests.

There is today an increased emphasis on the role of the laity, their gifts and the various ministries to which they are called.[30] As leaders of the faith community, priests exercise a significant dimension of their shepherding role through the support they offer the laity. As they encourage others to perform the tasks which are theirs by virtue of baptism, priests are called to provide vision, direction, and leadership. In doing so, they support the exercise of the gifts of the laity and encourage them to participate actively in building up the body of Christ.

The pastoral office of priests in its task of teaching, sanctifying, and leading is exercised not only on behalf of those explicitly committed to their priests' pastoral care but also on behalf of all men and women.[31] After the example of the Master, this shepherd's care must be performed with a missionary zeal toward all those who search for the truth.

As Jesus sent his followers to make disciples of all nations at the conclusion of the Gospel of Matthew, he promised to remain with them until the end of time.[32] And so Christ the high priest remains the living lord of the Church, sanctifying its life and mission by his presence. Christ dwells among us when the Word is proclaimed and the sacraments are celebrated, above all, in the eucharistic celebration. When Christians gather in his name, he is in their midst.[33] Christ the high priest is present in a special way in priests themselves as well as in their ministry. For this reason, ministry will have a profound effect on personal priestly life, becoming the path that priests follow as they seek to become holy themselves.[34]

Notes

1   PDV, no. 12; cf. PDV, nos. 11-18.

2   CL, no. 18.

3   Jn 3:16.

4   Jn 10:16.

5   The Second General Assembly of the Synod of Bishops, *The Ministerial Priesthood*, 1971, I, 1 (hereafter MP); cf. PDV, no. 13.

6   Heb 8:1-6; 9:11-14, 24-28; 10:11-14, 19-25.

7   MP, I, 1.

8   The Second Extraordinary General Assembly of the Synod of Bishops, *The Final Report*, 1985, II, A, 3 (hereafter TFR).

9   CL, no. 19; cf. TFR, II, C, 1, "The ecclesiology of communion is the central and fundamental idea of the council's documents" (PDV, no. 12).

10   LG, no. 7; Eph 4:7, 11-16; 1 Cor 12:13.

11   Cf. Mt 3:16; Lk 4:18; Acts 10:38; also PO, no. 2.

12   Cf. *Code of Canon Law* (CIC), cc. 204, 210-211; LG, nos. 10-12, 39-42; PO, no. 2; CL, no. 14.

13   PDV, no. 14.

14   *The Roman Pontifical* (ICEL, 1978) *Ordination of a Priest*, 14 (hereafter OP).

15   Rom 12:4; PO, no. 2.

16   LG, no. 10; PO, no. 2; cf. PDV, no. 15.

17   PDV, no. 16; cf. MP, I, 4.

18   LG, no. 10.

19   PDV, no. 16.

20   OP, no. 14.

21   PO, no. 4.

22   PO, no. 5; LG, no. 11; TFR, C, 1.

23   PDV, no. 11.

24   PO, no. 6.

25   PDV, no. 16.

26   PDV, no. 17; PO, no. 8.

27   PO, no. 2.

28   LG, no. 28; PO, no. 7.

29   Cf. Congregation for Institutes of Consecrated Life and Societies of Apostolic Life, "Mutual Relations," 1978, and "Directory on Formation in Religious Institutes," 1990.

30   LG, no. 43.

31   CL, nos. 23-25.

32   PDV, no. 18.

33   Mt 28:20.

34   Mt 18:20; cf. *Sacrosanctum Concilium*, no. 7.